FIPS

FIPS

Legendary U-Boat Commander
1915–1918

by
Werner Fürbringer

Translated from the German by
Geoffrey Brooks

NAVAL INSTITUTE PRESS
ANNAPOLIS, MARYLAND

Originally published as
Alarm! Touchen!! – U-Boot in Kampf und Sturm, Berlin, in 1933.

First published in Great Britain in 1999 by Leo Cooper,
an imprint of Pen & Sword Books, Ltd.,
47 Church Street, Barnsley, South Yorkshire S70 2AS.

Published and distributed in the United States of America
and Canada by the Naval Institute Press, 291 Wood Road,
Annapolis, Maryland 21402-5034

Library of Congress Catalog Card No. 99-69011
ISBN 1-55750-286-2

Printed in England

DEDICATION

I dedicate this book to two innocent victims of the Great War: to the dearly loved Fürbringer brother who as a private soldier in the German Army fell at Verdun on 31 May 1916; and to Mrs Mary Slaughter of Hebburn, a young lady visitor to the town of Seaham, who while taking a country walk in the company of a female relative on the evening of 12 July 1916 was hit by a shell fired by the German submarine *UB-39* and succumbed to her terrible injuries at Sunderland Hospital the following morning, the only casualty of the incident.

CONTENTS

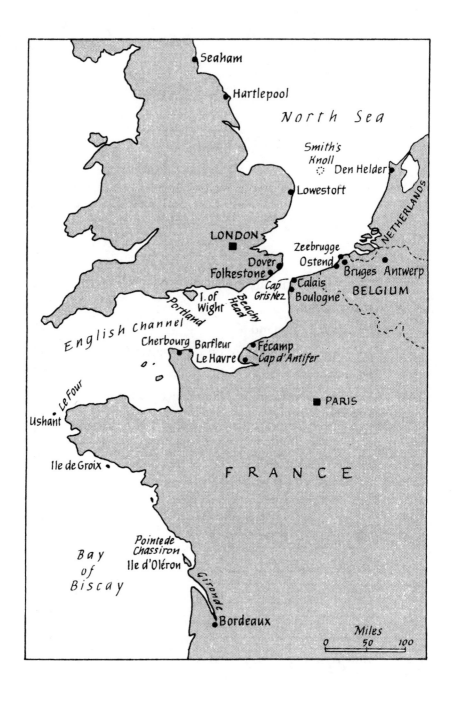

TRANSLATOR'S INTRODUCTION

Werner Fürbringer (b. Braunschweig 2 October 1888, d. 8 February 1982) was a career naval officer selected for the new U-boat Arm of the Imperial Navy. In the first six months of the Great War he served as first watchkeeping officer aboard *U-20* for two voyages under Otto Schwieger, immediately prior to the mission when the latter torpedoed the Cunarder *Lusitania* in May 1915.

Fürbringer was given his first command in April 1915 and from then until July 1918 operated out of the Bruges U-Boat base. No other submarine force in history has persevered with the 83% loss rate found acceptable by the Flanders U-Flotilla. Few officers survived to tell of their experiences and Fürbringer's memoir is probably unique.

In the desperate attempt to blockade Britain into surrender this small coastal submarine force wreaked havoc along the French and English coasts from Brest and Land's End to the Firth of Forth, minelaying and sinking by gun and torpedo all sizes of Allied vessel from troop transports to herring drifters.

It was a dangerous business and Fürbringer provides a frank account of the awesome dangers that awaited the U-boat commander as soon as his boat emerged beyond the mole at Zeebrugge: great minefields, searchlight barriers, mined net barriers, Q-ships in all disguises and armed lighthouses.

He was without doubt not only a very brave man but also a humane and chivalrous officer.

I am indebted for their invaluable assistance to Hans-Günther Fürbringer, his son, also to my old friends Wolfgang Hirschfeld of Plön in Holstein, former *Oberfunkmeister* in Doenitz' U-boat Arm, and to Philip Oastler of Southend-on-Sea, formerly of the British Merchant Navy, all of whom helped me with research and encouragement.

Geoffrey Brooks
Spain, 1999.

INTRODUCTION

I entered the Imperial German Navy as an officer cadet on 1 April 1907 at the age of eighteen. After receiving my commission I was drafted aboard the newly completed large cruiser *Scharnhorst*, flagship of the Far East Cruiser Squadron, and sailed aboard her for the German colony of Tsingtau in 1909.

I had my baptism of fire in 1912. As senior Leutnant of the flagship I was seconded to Oberleutnant Metzenthin of our sister ship *Gneisenau* and ordered to proceed aboard the German steamer *Titania* with a detachment of fifty men to the defence of the German settlers in the trading town of Hankau 1000 kilometres upstream. The 1912 Chinese Revolution had broken out. Directly behind the German settlement at Hankau there had been bloody fighting between the Imperial forces and the rebels, and for this reason our presence was urgently required for the protection of German lives, property and the flag. We were enthusiastic, but understandably apprehensive at the prospect of knowing war at first hand.

On the afternoon of the fourth day of the voyage, as the *Titania* passed Kiu-Kiang, then known worldwide for its porcelain vases, one of the town's forts hoisted a string of flags. The international semaphore books were consulted, but, as no sense could be made of the signal, it was decided to ignore it. When we had the town a mile astern five of the fort's guns opened fire.

1

There were some muzzle flashes and a thunderous crack. A few seconds later a salvo of shells howled over. I ducked instinctively below the bridge railings. It was my baptism of fire.

The Chinese were obviously serious. Our ship dropped anchor and the wireless operator attempted to contact the gunboat *Luchs* and other German warships lying upstream, but neither they nor the cruiser squadron seemed disposed to reply. Oberleutnant Metzenthin went ashore to lodge a protest with the British consul, who represented German diplomatic interests for the district, but the revolutionary fort commander was adamant and refused to allow *Titania* to proceed on the grounds that she was carrying ammunition for the Chinese Imperial forces. The following evening *Luchs* wirelessed instructions to threaten the fort with bombardment by German warships and at dawn the Chinese commander relented.

Our arrival in Hankau was cheered vociferously by the German colony. To our disappointment we learnt that the Imperial forces had withdrawn, thus depriving us of a first taste of battle. The fields behind the town were piled high with corpses. German sentries reported frequent attacks in the darkness by large wild dogs which evidently had found an appetite for human flesh. Mopping-up operations were therefore limited to destroying as many of these animals as possible.

We identified closely with the German colony. A splendid spirit characterized the trading community in Hankau. They worked grimly from dawn till dusk and cherished great hopes for the future. In a way they were over-dedicated to being entrepreneurs and neglected to enjoy life. Almost to the last man they had the single objective of making as much money as possible before ultimately returning to Germany. The British had a healthier attitude. They would shut up shop early and keep fit and well with sport. Many of them had been in China for generations and were quite happy to settle there. Naturally they took a dim view of business being conducted at a brisker tempo than their own!

After six months at Hankau a relief party arrived and we returned to our beautiful, proud model colony of Tsingtau. The cruiser squadron embarked upon its 1912 summer voyage, calling at Japanese ports, the island of Sakhalin and anchoring in a number of bays on the coast of Eastern Siberia.

In August 1912 *Scharnhorst* had just anchored at Nagasaki. While supervising work on the fo'c'sle I noticed a naval pinnace come alongside to deliver the latest telegrams from Berlin. Shortly afterwards the commander called down to me from the bridge, "Congratulations, Fürbringer, you've been selected for U-boats!" I had become the first officer to be selected for transfer into submarines from the cruiser squadron. Everybody seemed very excited about it in the wardroom and I was roundly congratulated. Privately I was unsure whether it was to be considered a distinction, but evidently my colleagues envied me.

I entrained at Vladivostok for Germany via Moscow and travelled through the bleak snowscape of a Siberian winter. Many races of mankind thronged the railway platforms. It was December 1912; war had broken out in the Balkans. At nearly every large station between Harbin and Moscow we passed troop transport trains heading west!

Aboard the old *U-1* and on the modern *U-20* I learnt the art of U-boat handling. The CO of the Half-Flotilla, Gayer, kept the service under a tight rein and training was maintained at a relentless pace. He was intent upon having the newest boats worked up to a level footing with the veteran vessels. This gave us a hard life, but we soon noticed our improved standard and it was not long before we were on a par with the older boats. In May 1914 we participated in the North Sea naval exercises with the High Seas Fleet. Despite severe gales, we gave a creditable account of ourselves and provided the Planning Staff with an idea of what was to be expected of us if the need arose.

My annual leave coincided with Kiel Week. I went to stay with my mother in the Harz, in a forester's house at Oker near Harzburg. On the afternoon of Sunday 28 June, when I went down into the town to collect the newspapers and mail, I learnt of the assassination of the heir to the Austrian throne. When I told my mother, she wept as if she knew what that portended. I returned at once to Kiel.

In the wardroom aboard the U-boat depot ship *Acheron* the

3

possibility of war was much discussed, but still nobody thought it would come immediately. When we gave the matter serious thought in those July days of 1914 we imagined a short, victorious two-front campaign in which it would fall to the Imperial German Navy to take on the French and Russian Fleets. When the Chief of Staff, U-boats, ordered all officers to remain in reach at all times either directly or by telephone, then we knew that war was almost certain. The Half-Flotilla CO, who wanted his U-boats to be ready for any eventuality, ordered the torpedo warheads to be shipped. A certain number of officers were even required to sleep aboard the submarines from now on. This was at the end of July 1914. By then I was first watchkeeping officer of *U-20*.

I remember well the air of great excitement at Kiel on the day when the Kaiser ordered "increased security". All naval vessels were dressed with the semaphore "All men report aboard"; sirens howled constantly and the noise was deafening. Landing stages and accommodation ladders shuddered and swayed beneath enthusiastic crowds of naval crewmen.

It was a glorious summer's day when the Third Half-Flotilla slipped its moorings alongside the *Acheron*. Wherever we passed there were scenes of jubilation. Dear friends waved to us. When would we see them again? Cruising through the Kiel Canal, we saw boundless enthusiasm.

At dawn we crossed the Elbe Estuary for Wilhelmshaven. Next afternoon the Jade receded astern as we made for the North Sea island of Heligoland. At 2230 hrs the same evening, halfway there, we took down a wireless message from our leader boat: "Dowse lights at once. War has broken out with Russia and France. Do not attack English ships." Unlit, the flotilla boat ploughed on for Heligoland. We were at war. And soon we would be at war with Britain too.

On 5 August 1914, the day following the outbreak of war with Britain, U-boats were stationed in a protective belt on both sides of Heligoland close in to the coast. The British were expected to make an attack at any moment. It was a time of false alarms. The endless waiting made us jittery. The uncertainty as to what lay ahead made the tension worse.

Everybody wanted the first clash with the enemy so as to clear the air.

On 28 August 1914 the British struck unexpectedly. The light cruisers *Mainz*, *Köln*, *Ariadne* and a torpedo-boat were sunk and we lost a thousand lives. Next morning a light cruiser put into the torpedo-boat basin, her aft funnel battered by shelling. For me it was the first visible sign of the enemy's existence. The adverse effect of the action on our morale, the so-called Battle of the Heligoland Bight, was immense. We had lost four ships without reply in a daring coup and one had to give the enemy full credit for the careful reconnaissance and planning which must have gone into it.

The U-boats took the lesson to heart. A few days later *U-20* and *U-21* were detailed to penetrate the Firth of Forth and cause havoc. On the evening of 5 September *U-21* sank the light cruiser *Pathfinder*, but my boat *U-20* returned empty handed.

At the beginning of October *U-20* was sent to Boulogne to attack the Canadian troop transports which regularly put into the port. The enemy had freshly mined the stretch of seaway between the Thames Estuary and the Flanders coast, but we slipped through the barrage unscathed. Naturally we were overjoyed at this success and set ourselves to the mission with enthusiasm. However, no troop transports showed up. After a few days lying in abortive ambush the commander cursed his luck and took us to Cherbourg. Here he remained unrewarded. On the English side of the Channel the nearer we got the worse grew the visibility. It was very misty indeed.

The only piece of good luck on the voyage was to survive a ramming attempt by a British destroyer in fog near the Isle of Wight. After consulting the watchkeeping officers and coxswain the commander decided to return home by the north-about route instead of through the Channel. We had sufficient fuel, and the thick mists which had been developing would certainly have made the passage of the Dover Straits and the mine barrage a difficult undertaking. The commander took the view that possibly other British coasts offered better prospects for success than the Channel. We steered for Land's End over the Lizard and then northwards through the Irish Sea.

Off the northern tip of Ireland we were buffeted for a while by a NW gale. This soon slackened off, but a huge swell persisted for several days.

As we approached the Hebrides on the surface from the south, visibility was very hazy and heavy squalls shrouded much of the horizon. Suddenly the lookouts glimpsed the top hamper of several major warships. The commander said they were modern battleships or battle-cruisers. The Royal Navy considered its ships so safe in these waters that they had not bothered to arrange destroyer protection for the squadron. No German U-Boat commander would ever obtain an opportunity like this again. Unfortunately *U-20* could not be trimmed at periscope depth in the sea conditions. In this case, as in all the others, luck had been against the commander once more. We felt sick at heart. The navigator plotted a course north around Scotland and then through the Skagerrak. The port engine broke down and we limped home at a very slow speed. Eleven days after sailing *U-20* returned to Heligoland. The length of our voyage was a source of admiration, but that was little consolation for another blank scoresheet.

U-20 gained a new commander, Kapitänleutnant Otto Schwieger. He was to prove a high-scoring U-boat commander in terms of tonnage sunk and his name is probably better known to the casual reader than those of De la Perière, Valentiner, Hersing and Hashagen, who all outperformed him. I served as Schwieger's first watchkeeping officer until March 1915. In that time, operating from Emden, we made two long and very successful patrols through the Channel and as far north as Liverpool.

For some time German Naval Command had suspected the abuse of the Red Cross Convention by Great Britain. While returning from the second of these voyages in February 1915, Schwieger attempted unsuccessfully to torpedo a hospital ship approaching the French port of Le Havre, her decks and rails crowded with armed British troops bound for the Front. I could hardly believe my eyes and confirmed Schwieger's own observation through the periscope before the attack was made. The incident was fully reported in the *U-20* War Diary.

Putting into Emden after completing the second patrol in

early March 1915 our Half-Flotilla CO, Gayer congratulated me on having been given command of a small UB-Type boat.

As Schwieger shook my hand and gave me his best wishes, I felt no elation, even though my dream was about to be fulfilled, for it was only now that I realized how much the gallant *U-20*, and more so her commander, meant to me. Fate brings the parting of the ways, and all that remained was to be grateful for the time I had spent at sea with this outstanding commander and splendid person. One must speak as one finds. A watch officer could not have wished for a more ideal collaboration than that which I had experienced with Schwieger. What would I say were the qualities of Kapitänleutnant Schwieger? Noble-mindedness. An even temperament. Sensitivity. Determination. A lively mind. And last but not least a sense of humour which never deserted him. All these made the partnership with him, especially on patrol, an experience. My ideas coincided so exactly with his that I would nearly always know in advance what he was proposing to do, and accordingly we acted in harmony. If I now had to part from him, the separation would be physical only: his example would always be the guiding principle on all my future missions.

After a short lay-up *U-20* moved down to Wilhelmshaven for engine repairs, and it was there that our real leave-taking took place. In a quiet corner of a wine-bar Schwieger had arranged a farewell dinner for the four officers of *U-20*; at my place I found a silver cigarette case engraved with the letters of the famous semaphore message:

D	Ü	Ö
N	U	F
Ä	K	T
Ä	P	Z

which means "Warmest thanks for loyal cooperation".

In a short speech Schwieger referred to my service aboard *U-20* in terms that made me blush, and, mentioning our parting, made a few pithy and humorous remarks which defused the emotion of the event. Then. . . . farewell for ever. I never saw him again. We kept in touch by correspondence until one day my letter was returned, laconically stamped "Missing". He had failed to return from patrol.

Translator's Note

Perhaps the most oft-quoted example of alleged German "frightfulness" at sea is the sinking of the Cunard liner *Lusitania* by Otto Schwieger in *U-20* about 12 miles off the Old Head of Kinsale in the early afternoon of 7 May 1915. 1198 persons, a number of them neutral Americans, perished in the disaster. Fürbringer was not aboard *U-20* at the time: *Lusitania* was sunk on the patrol following his transfer to the U-boat commanders' course.

In a reply made under interrogation while a British prisoner in 1918, Fürbringer stated that he would also have sunk the *Lusitania*. The incident at Seaham recounted later in this book shows how he took unusual measures to spare civilians, and so his assertion suggests that there was a definite political reason for sinking the liner.

Principally on account of the grave nitrate shortage, on 4 February 1915 Admiral von Tirpitz convinced the German Government as to the immediate necessity of unrestricted submarine warfare and the Chief of the German Naval Staff, Admiral von Pohl, issued a warning countersigned by the Kaiser that:

> "the waters surrounding Great Britain and Ireland [all one country at war with Germany in 1915], including the whole English Channel, are hereby declared to be a war zone. On or after 18th February 1915 every enemy merchant ship found in the said war zone will be destroyed without its being always possible to avert the danger threatening the crews and *passengers* on that account."

This was a declaration of unrestricted submarine warfare within the specific area mentioned. Germany was within sight of defeat. "Every merchant vessel" meant precisely that.

The *Lusitania* was a British flag vessel bound for the Mersey and found in the waters surrounding Ireland. She was capable of carrying rifles, explosives, war contraband and enemy personnel. Whether she was doing so or not was immaterial.

Schwieger was a professional naval officer. He would have discussed the hospital ship incident at policy level on his return to Germany in March 1915 and sought guidance, if such were needed, on the interpretation of von Pohl's warning and very probably his

8

personal secret orders. The connection between the alleged abuse of hospital ships by Britain, as confirmed by Schwieger, and the deliberate naval policy of sinking passenger liners, as commenced by Schwieger, cannot be dismissed lightly. Much has been written about Otto Schwieger's demeanour at the crucial moment and the inference drawn that his was a purely personal decision to boost his tonnage figures. But it is surely much more likely, when he saw what he dreaded to see, the four funnels hoving into view off the Old Head of Kinsale, that he had long known the identity of this ship, and knew too that the terrible thing he had been ordered to do would result in his being condemned for ever at the bar of history. Such is the burden of command. Admiral von Pohl's order was rescinded after the *Lusitania* sinking as the result of diplomatic pressure.

That passenger liners must have been legitimate targets within the meaning of the 1915 order is to be inferred from the personal diary of Admiral Hipper, Fleet C-in-C from August 1918. He recorded on 19 October 1918 "the very depressing information that the German Government was strongly inclined to give in to all President Wilson's demands including the cessation of attacks on passenger liners. This would mean the end of the U-boat war altogether, of course." The following day the matter was placed in the hands of the Kaiser for his decision, together with advice that "if the U-boat War was continued but passenger ships were to be spared, this would so effectively impair the prosecution of the U-boat War as to render it meaningless." At nine that evening the Kaiser informed Admiral Scheer "with the deepest regret" that he saw no alternative but to accede to the demand of the Government in the matter. "Thereafter U-boats were not to attack passenger ships under any circumstances," Admiral Hipper wrote, "KptzS von Levetzow advised me that this was the end of the U-boat War."

(The text of Admiral Hipper's diaries appears in *Die Schweren Kreuzer der Admiral Hipper-Klasse*, Koop & Schmolke Bernard & Graefe Verlag, Bonn, 1992.)

Chapter One

MY FIRST COMMAND

I took command of *UB-2* at the end of March 1915 and endured the arduous month-long training period at the U-boat School to earn the coveted description "Fit for the front" (*frontreif*). As a reward, at the beginning of May I received an especially important mission.

UB-2 and her sister boats had been allocated to the Belgian coast, but were so small and underpowered that it was believed the only way to get them there from Germany was by rail. For this purpose they were reduced to three component parts, brought to Antwerp by goods train and re-assembled prior to making the difficult inland canal passage to Bruges. From Bruges it was then a simple matter to get to the open sea via the Bruges-Zeebrugge Canal.

As all this dismantling and re-assembly work took up a great deal of valuable time for all concerned I was detailed to pioneer the sea route from Germany round the coast of the neutral Netherlands to Flanders. This didn't seem a very difficult task; I had got to know my boat very well during the working-up period and had an idea of her capabilities. Therefore I saw no problem. Others preferred to differ. Their opinion was based primarily on the constructional details of *UB-2* which were admittedly not impressive. The boat was 27 metres in length and displaced 120 tonnes. Both propulsion systems, a diesel and an electric motor, developed 60 hp which provided a maximum speed of five knots surfaced in a calm sea or submerged. The diesel had been originally designed for a naval pinnace. The crew numbered thirteen men. When this data was compared with that of other warships, such as torpedo-boats for instance, as a number of colleagues were apt to do, then their doubts were understandable, but even so it didn't bother me.

In a wine bar at Masius I bade farewell to my eldest brother, Gerhardt, commander of the large submarine *U-40*. Five years of trial and tribulation would pass before our next reunion.* I had orders to put to sea unnoticed at 0130 hrs and proceed through the Kiel Canal for Borkum from where I would sail for Flanders.

UB-2 made a discreet navigation of the Kiel Canal and by morning reached Cuxhaven where four torpedo-boats took us under tow to Borkum Roads. A ridiculously fast speed was maintained throughout this latter operation and we expected to capsize or be dragged under at any moment. All weather stations on the North Sea coast were concentrating on the conditions likely to affect *UB-2* during the onward passage and we received hourly reports. From these it appeared that the weather would be favourable.

I was hoping to put out from Borkum alone but my former Chief, Gayer, wouldn't hear of it and I was dismayed to learn that his old torpedo-boat would tow us seawards for a stretch. Again a fast speed was considered suitable and we were dragged out in a great flurry of foam and spray. Suddenly some smudges of smoke appeared off the bow. Gayer suspected it might be a superior British naval force, and without further ado, his boat simply threw off the 200-metre-long tow-line and headed at full speed for Borkum. We were left to contemplate the disposal of the massive steel hawser hanging down from our stem. It was so heavy that the eye couldn't be lifted over the bollard and in the

---

* On 23 June 1915 *U-40* became the first U-boat to fall prey to a decoy trawler towing a submerged submarine. Gerhardt Fürbringer and his coxswain were the only survivors to be found by the trawler *Taranaki* when *U-40* was torpedoed by HM S/M C-24.

end we had to hack it free with a hammer and chisel.

I heaved a sigh of relief that we had rid ourselves of this damned dangerous towing nonsense. I wondered at the lack of nautical expertise exhibited by our torpedo-boat commanders and was glad they were all safely back in port. I turned on our little engine and we sputtered off happily at four knots towards the black smudges on the western horizon.

The smoke was not Britain's Grand Fleet but a group of neutral Dutch trawlers. I set course without further incident for Den Helder and then bore round to the south. During the night a heavy swell got up from the north-west. The meteorologists, who had promised us the finest weather for the trip, had deceived us: the Naval Corps knew the boat could sail in light airs, obviously what they really needed to know was how it handled in an unexpected Force Ten. At first light the wind began to strengthen: by midday it was blowing at storm force.

At first the seas merely towered up astern to sweep forward over the conning tower, and with these the boat coped bravely, but as the great liquid ridges grew more mountainous and confused the small submarine pitched and yawed at all kinds of strange angles, once giving me a real fright when she slewed round almost broadside. The shaking put the gyro-compass out. Our reserve, the magnetic compass on the bridge, was also out of commission: the glass disc had misted up on the inside and the card couldn't be read. The night was as black as pitch, the storm howled and the wind raged. I decided to put the boat on the ground and gave the order to submerge.

In the steep seas the dive was a neck-breaking manoeuvre. *UB-2* headed precipitately for the sea bed and struck heavily. The effects of the storm were violent even at 28 metres and could only be countered by giving the boat a nose-heavy trim so that the bow rested on the bottom while the remainder of the hull was balanced at an angle upwards. As much of the sea-water ballast as possible was expelled to reduce the jarring movement of the swell: it could not be eliminated completely but was transformed into a relatively light feathering kind of motion. We kept this trim until morning.

13

After a twelve-hour buffeting we surfaced to find a fresh breeze and a wonderful blue sky. We had no usable compass and plotted a track by the sun: within three hours the Dutch coast was visible on the port hand. I decided to follow it all the way down to Zeebrugge.

A submarine surfaced and ordered me out of Dutch territorial waters: I obeyed while steering a course that gradually brought me back under the coast without the Dutchman detecting it. *UB-2* proceeded undisturbed until midday when a German U-boat hove in sight directly ahead. This was *UB-4*, which the Chief of the Flanders Flotilla, Korvettenkapitän Bartenbach, had sent out to escort us through the German minefields on the Belgian coast.

We made Zeebrugge that afternoon, berthing an hour later at Bruges, to be received by the Flotilla Chief and the representative of the Naval Corps. That evening Bartenbach made a speech of welcome in the officers' club. I was informed that my exploit would not be forgotten lightly.

And so the spell was broken, and successive boats came round from Germany by sea, thus enabling the strength of the Flanders U-boat Flotilla to be greatly augmented month by month.

The coast was in a constant state of alert for surprise landings by the British. Belgian Flanders was protected by countless artillery emplacements, but it was still considered a worthwhile precaution always to have a couple of small U-boats on station just off the coast. This sentry duty was much deprecated as there was rarely, if ever, any contact with the enemy, yet we were obliged to remain in a state of the highest alertness at all times.

Every day we expected the British to make an appearance but they had no inclination to come over.

Our Flotilla Chief began to edge us farther and farther offshore until finally his bagful of U-boats went across the North Sea to *them*: finally we were operating off the English coast itself. Now at last we felt we were real U-boatmen: now we could get busy in the murderous manner we had dreamed of all these weeks and months!

* * *

14

"I think you have the most lovely eyes," Oberleutnant Valentiner told me. I was taken somewhat aback. "I'm going to have some painted on my boat too, above a shark-mouth." My friend had meant the eyes of my boat *UB-2* now lying in the yards at Bruges. I had had a black-white-red roundel stuck each side of the bow well forward to serve as an identification symbol. The eyes, together with the pronounced convex nose of *UB-2*, gave the boat a rather whale-like appearance. Valentiner's boat with eyes and shark's mouth would definitely look like some kind of sea monster. However, I had more urgent business to attend to than boats' markings, for tomorrow we were to sail on a special operation. We had often splashed about in *UB-2* off the English south-east coast, but now we had a real mission – we were to be unleashed in the English Channel itself!

The life artery of Britain, the English Channel, ebbed and flowed directly at our Belgian doorstep. Nevertheless Bartenbach had not been able to make the decision to deploy his flotilla there while the doubt existed as to whether our small submarines were technically up to the task. We were aware of his burning desire to extend operations into the Channel if at all possible. He had not had long to wait, for the proof he required, dispelling all doubts, was supplied by Operation Haecker.

Reports had been received that the enemy had sealed the Straits of Dover by means of anti-submarine nets which stretched from Dover to Calais. The investigation of the matter had fallen to Oberleutnant Haecker, and on completion of this dangerous mission he had been able to report that, whereas the Straits were almost totally netted off, there was a definite gap close under the French coast between Calais and Cap Gris-Nez. So now we received our operational orders.

UB-2 and three similar boats were to take station one each off the Channel ports of Dover, Folkestone, Boulogne and Le Havre, to expend their torpedoes on enemy troop transports and supply ships and then beat a hasty retreat. I had been allotted Le Havre, which was the farthest distant. I took pride that my boat had been awarded this honour. *UB-2* had been the first boat of the Flotilla to come down to Flanders from

15

Germany by the sea route: the other boats had been brought overland in parts and re-assembled at Antwerp. *UB-2* was a proven voyager.

"My heartiest best wishes," Bartenbach said. We left Bruges on the evening of a blistering July day. It took us just an hour to complete the passage of the canal to Zeebrugge and the weather was still sultry as *UB-2* put to sea. The coast dwindled from sight and when night fell we steered west. No mishap befell us before locating Haecker's gap in the anti-submarine netting next day but while negotiating it on the surface we were forced to submerge when disturbed by an approaching destroyer. Subsequently it passed overhead but disappeared without animosity. I judged it safe to return to the surface within a few minutes and then headed for Cap Gris-Nez. Just off the point, where the narrowest part of the Strait suddenly broadens into the Channel proper, we were met by the full force of the counter-current. Our diesel was running full out and roared so loud that I thought it impossible for the British patrol vessels in the near neighbourhood not to hear it in the calm night air, but apparently it failed to disturb their slumbers. Our screw thrashed furiously for hours and managed no more than to keep us rooted in the same spot. Abruptly, almost with a perceptible jolt, the flow ceased, and we began to make progress in the required direction. With our underpowered engine we had spent four hours marking time off the dangerous headland.

By dusk next evening we lay between Beachy Head and Cape Antifer: the Antifer light was just visible above the horizon and this signified our arrival in the operational area ordered. The voyage here had taken a little longer than anticipated and I proposed wasting no more time. We would start at once! *UB-2* settled in ambush. Little time passed before a deeply laden supply ship hove in sight from the direction of the English coast. What was her cargo? Munitions for the Western Front? A fine target!

A torpedo was readied quickly before she could escape us. The night was not dark and it was calm. *UB-2* crept up within range on the electric motor. I fired – waited – waited – nothing. Missed! It had been a sitting duck: the torpedo must have gone

16

beneath her keel. To be sure of hitting, I had gone in too close. At very short range the torpedo ran below the depth set.

I perched on the bridge with the coxswain and boatswain. The boat rolled gently. We gazed in silence at the fat ship steaming unconcernedly onwards for Le Havre. Momentarily I thought about giving chase and firing the second torpedo at her stern. But our top speed was 5 knots while the steamer was making ten. Our pitiful engine power!

Well, the torpedo had been wasted and I had to live with it. What's gone is gone, but how heartsick I felt about it! But we still had one torpedo, and on this rested our hopes of returning home with at least a 50% success rate. For the time being, however, I had lost my taste for night action. It seemed a more reliable proceeding to loose off the second torpedo in a surface attack by day.

For the remainder of the night the boat lay on the bottom and we slept. A fog, grey and thick, was found to be shrouding the surface at 0500; from time to time during the day I checked to see whether it had lifted but not until dawn the following day did it clear, revealing a cloudless sky. This promised a glorious day, made for an attack! In the distance I could see the cliffs at Antifer and knew we were in the right position. The sun rose almost purplish-gold and visibility was excellent. I submerged so as to avoid detection.

Less than an hour had passed when a large transport came up in our direction. I recognized the red ensign. Prepare torpedo! I had completed the mathematical calculations but one minute before the firing time the steamer's heading changed towards us. This forced me to cross his bows to attempt the shot from his other side. This took so long to achieve that by the time I could take another peep at him through the periscope from our new position his stern was passing us. I aimed, fired and retracted the periscope. When I glanced at the periscope bearing indicator I noticed that the line of aim showed 18 degrees to starboard. It should have been eighteen degrees to port. On crossing to the other side of the target no adjustment had been made! The torpedo would miss! It missed.

"Why didn't you reset the indicator, coxswain?"

The small portly warrant officer answered calmly, his voice reproachful, "When the Herr Oberleutnant kept swivelling with the periscope, he crushed me so much against the bulkhead that I couldn't get round to the compass. Also when I was squashed I got caught on a hook and tore open the seat of my pants." In the control room somebody spluttered. Then we all laughed.

Coxswain Becker was right. When we were both in the conning tower, there was no room to move, yet when making a torpedo attack the presence of us both was required there. It wasn't easy for Becker. I had to work at the periscope, climb up and down, circle round and round and always squashed up against him: sometimes when accidentally I put a knee into his fat midriff he would groan deeply, but for all that we remained on good terms.

I felt weak at the knees. Both torpedoes wasted. It was wretched luck. The men had slaved to get the boat here safely, and I had fired wide twice. What would the Flotilla Chief say? And the other three commanders? How they would amuse themselves at my expense! I stood in the tower, slumped against the bulkhead, brooding. Thoughts chased each other through my head. This was bad: I was in the blackest humour. It was quiet in the boat, almost like a ghost ship: nothing but the gentle humming of the electric motors and an occasional whispered order to the hydroplane operators. I had handed the periscope watch to the coxswain. Suddenly he startled me out of my deliberations. "Steamer gone, nothing in sight!"

I took over, checked his report and surfaced. The coxswain handed me the chart. "Course for home 65 degrees, Herr Oberleutnant!"

"Then let's go," I said. "Start up the diesel!"

The engine telegraph rattled. For a moment nothing happened, then there was a short sigh, followed by a jolt which rocked the boat. The engine died.

"What's up?" I asked.

"We can't tell yet, Herr Oberleutnant," came the reply.

Fifteen minutes passed, then acting ERA Hausmann appeared at the tower with an ashen face. "The coupling between the diesel and electric motors is broken, Herr Oberleutnant. We can only sail on the batteries."

"How long will the repair take?"

"If the repair is actually possible with the tools at our disposal on board, at least four days."

"So we must assume that it is not possible. How much charge is there in the batteries?"

"At half speed, enough for three to four hours, Herr Oberleutnant."

That was enough for ten to twelve sea miles but it was 120 miles to Zeebrugge or Ostend. 'My heartiest best wishes' indeed! This was turning out to be a nice little trip. First we miss with both torpedoes and now we had no main engine. How were we supposed to get back? And what would we have to eat and drink on the way?

I looked around. The wind had dropped completely, the sea was like a mirror. To the farthest horizon there was nothing in sight. I stood on the bridge with my two warrant officers, pale-faced ERA Hausmann and coxswain Becker, corpulent and reserved. We spoke in an undertone; there was no need for everybody to be party to our deliberations. We were in a very ticklish spot. Summing up the situation the only possibility open to us was to allow ourselves to be borne up-Channel by the current.

After a few moments the plan was agreed upon: we would drift with the current up to the Calais nets: that is, we would drift on the surface when the flood was eastwards, and sit it out on the bottom when it ebbed westwards. In the latter case it would have been preferable to anchor instead of rest on the ground, but we would need to submerge at the approach of enemy patrols and the task of raising the anchor on *UB-2* was a heavy and dangerous one. Twice a day on the ebb, therefore, two periods of six hours each, in order to resist being driven back down-Channel, we had no option but to sit it out on the bottom awaiting the favourable current. Our calculations showed that we should be able to advance eight to ten sea miles eastwards twice daily and so reach the nets at Calais after four days. Until then we would forget we had a reserve of electric current in the batteries. This was our only hope of negotiating Haecker's Gap, which was the trickiest part of the whole voyage. From here to the nets four days: from the nets to Zeebrugge another four days, eight in all. What was the position with the provisions?

"The eggs are off," Becker cursed. I ordered the No. 2 boatswain to make an inventory and report. There was little left of the fresh provisions: the iron rations consisted of black bread and canned meat and vegetables. This was sufficient for three normal days. But the food concerned me less than the water situation, which was very serious. We had experienced some hot days which had led to excessive water consumption. We had expected to be home in three days: what remained had to last us eight, one cup of water daily per man. There would be no tea, coffee or anything warm; the electricity had to be conserved for the passage of the Gap. The cook had left the oil cooker ashore at Bruges because it took up too much space in our narrow tube. Therefore we faced the prospect of a cold buffet, the rations being reduced to a third, and one cup of water per day.

"Men," I said to the crew, "you know how it stands with us. Take in your belts one more notch to keep out the pangs of hunger and we'll make it." We were all convinced that we would. I was personally very confident, *UB-2* had a young crew. The unexpected and the dangerous were a challenge to us.

The current set westwards: it was time to submerge for the first spell on the sea bed. The hatch was dogged shut and we were soon down. In that there was nothing unusual. If we didn't know that the boat was submerged, normally we couldn't tell. But now we could. Nobody remarked, but everybody felt, how less snug it was than before. It was almost completely dark. The tube was small, only 27 metres long. But it seemed that the control room in which most of us found ourselves now was endlessly long, like a subterranean corridor, or the shaft of a coalmine. Somewhere astern in the engine room a small bulb glowed, the only light in the boat. Nevertheless it was still as dark as a potato cellar, and as stuffy.

Was this the same control room once so confined yet snug?

20

Dark figures stole past: some were recognizable, others not. It seemed in this darkness that the distance between each person was somehow greater, that the bond which united the thirteen men of *UB-2* had somehow been loosened. I felt suddenly more lonely than before. My mind, restless, could not be stilled. I was assailed by strange concepts and old memories long forgotten. I battled to think of realities.

If we could use the batteries now, this control room would be a flood of light. The air purification system would be running. The air we were breathing was now foul, and far worse than we were prepared to admit. A small quantity of oxygen had been released into the boat and we assured each other that it was doing some good, but the delusion was short-lived. Gradually we began to gasp for breath.

Ever more frequently I glanced at the clock. The first four hours of this misery were behind us; only another two hours to go. If my calculations were correct, we had to endure another eight 6-hour periods of darkness and dyspnoea. What would we not have given to go up for air right then! Another two hours, then one hour more, the longest.

Finally the tidal stream reversed. We surfaced, the ghastly hours suddenly forgotten in glorious sunshine, and a fresh breeze from the west in which we pumped our lungs full of clean, fresh air. Coxswain Becker had a scheme to rig a sail. This would give us the benefit of the westerly wind as well as the eastward current. A wonderful idea! Feverishly we set to, and in a trice we had a square-sail cobbled together out of canvas hammocks and bent to a number of boathooks. Once rigged it worked! When we drifted on the tide, it appeared that we were at a standstill even though we knew that we were making a few knots, but now our progress through the water was evident and the helm had to be manned to keep His Germanic Majesty's sailing submarine *UB-2* pointing in the required direction. We were tireless and confident. On deck everybody found himself work; the time for sitting propped up in some corner, hands in pockets, belonged in the 6-hour period below.

In the engine room Hausmann and his gang, consisting of

machinist-mate Döring, Petty Officer stoker Müller and stoker Hartig, laboured over the coupling; perhaps it could be repaired, they hinted, perhaps in less than four days. From below I heard an energetic knocking and hammering. Hausmann and his team? No, other engine-room personnel soon appeared on deck with two oars fashioned from bed boards. They had sacrificed their bunks in the effort to help. To atone for the failure of their department, they explained. As we had no rowlocks the oars were secured with ropework. The men took the matter very seriously. I devised a rota system for the oars and helm. Did the oars help much? Of course! I am not so sure that they added very much to our speed through the water, but it gave the men an incentive not to lie around doing nothing the whole day. In fact sail and oar augmented our speed by two knots.

After a couple of hours a destroyer was seen hull-down on the horizon but on a heading that would give us a wide berth. I decided to remain on the surface since at this distance he would be certain to mistake us for a fishing vessel, but even so it gave me a slightly uneasy feeling to have our natural enemy patrolling past and in sight relatively near. Ever mindful of not using the batteries unnecessarily, I was determined to keep my nerve and not submerge.

After some minutes the destroyer started to head in our general direction; he was not bearing down on us directly but would pass us on a parallel course nearby. Had he become suspicious of us for some reason and wanted a closer look? I was in a quandary, for if he recognized us as a U-boat and turned to attack, I would have no option but to dive with the sailing rig standing. I could imagine ways in which the tackle might betray our submerged position, or the propeller might get tangled up in the saturated sail canvas, neither being desirable from my point of view!

I decided to let him approach to within 3 kilometres. If he wasn't completely blind he was bound to see what we were round about that distance. When he was only that far off, I accepted that we had to submerge and ordered the electric motors for minimum revolutions so as not to have the sail ripped down during the descent. A very shallow dive was executed to disguise the manoeuvre from the destroyer. We lay on the bottom and waited, listening to the propellor noises growing fainter – and then silence.

On surfacing half an hour later the destroyer could just be made out on the horizon. The jury rig had survived the immersion and I gave the helmsman our course.

To my dismay the wind soon fell away, leaving our sail hanging listlessly and I had it stowed. The July sun beat down mercilessly on the iron segments of the deck and one could not walk there barefoot. In the interior of the boat it was unpleasantly hot. The current switched; it was time to wait on the seabed. We all knew what that meant. We hyperoxygenated at the surface, but that is a mere figure of speech – the lungs have no capacity for storing a reserve. The boat could not be ventilated because that consumed electricity from the batteries. After three hours the panting began.

Water! Water! If only there were any to spare! But each man had been given his daily cupful on deck, for today there was no more. The tongue stuck to the palate and water dominated all our thinking. A little oxygen was released into the boat but failed to alleviate our distress in any degree. In other circumstances the electric fans would be humming furiously now, circulating the air through potash cartridges which absorbed the poisonous carbon dioxide content of rebreathed air. In our present emergency we had to hold the cartridge directly in front of the mouth and breathe through it. This needed all one's attention.

The potash cartridge was tasteless but when used to effect it got very hot; after a short period one couldn't bear to place the lips on it, and when later it really heated up it couldn't even be held in the hand. The best remedy was to wrap it in a handkerchief soaked in seawater. We still breathed hot air, but at least it was mild and purified. The mouth, nostrils and breathing passages became increasingly more dry.

Hausmann and Döring achieved the impossible during these periods under water. As they needed both hands free for the work, they were unable to use their cartridges. They were perpetually gasping for breath in so sterterous a manner that this gave rise to continuing concern for their well-being. However, they made it clear that they would not be prised loose from their undertaking even if it killed them. When the boat was surfaced, the four of them were rarely to be seen on deck, preferring to toil below at the broken coupling. I had given the strictest orders that as soon as we came up I wanted the entire crew, and particularly Hausmann and his gang, on deck. Usually they would make the briefest appearance and then quietly slink off to the engine-room once more. We had fresh air, they had a fresh will, and – their work. In our relative idleness we envied them. Doing next to nothing was almost as exhausting as toil.

All in all the second day was tolerable. We were beginning to adjust to the torment while our anticipation of the adventure ahead kept morale high. Navigational fixes proved our steady eastwards drift towards the high point of the voyage, the passage of Haecker's Gap.

When the boat surfaced on the third day the sun was so hot that it left us almost prostrate with exhaustion. There was no hint of a wind and no point in raising the sail. I had quietly allowed the rowing to be abandoned. The crew were weaker physically than hitherto for lack of food and water.

The tidal stream turned, compelling our return to the bottom in the confines of our submersible dungeon. Below, there was a fearsome atmosphere. Clearly something was amiss. On attempting to oxygenate the air it was discovered that the supply pipe had a small fracture through which the gas was escaping: already a large quantity had been lost. The leak was soon located and sealed but oxygen was now added to the list of things we didn't have much of. The slightest movement made by any of the thirteen bodies in the boat reduced the oxygen reserve further and I was forced to issue the instruction that while submerged everybody but the four engine-room machinists had to remain immobile and mute. Breathing was permitted, but no other activity. Accordingly from the third day onwards our fear of the 6-hour ordeal below grew steadily.

One would sit silently in some convenient dark spot or stand propped against a bulkhead, morosely contemplating the horror whose arrival was soon due. First came the stifling sensation, then resignation as the dyspnoea set in. It would affect some earlier than others, but in the end none escaped. The potash cartridge would be raised to the mouth; it seemed as though it got hotter much quicker than before. Mouth, pharynx and nasal passages burnt with dryness; three breaths were taken where previously in the ordeal one had sufficed. Gradually the strain on the heart could be felt and this caused an inner panic, a perpetual funk that the body wouldn't be able to take it much more. How much longer could one hold out? And twice daily for six hours waiting in this clammy tube, in this hell!

My gaze would wander down to the little work lamp glowing at the very end of the boat, in the engine-room where Hausmann was working on the coupling. Could they do it, those brave men? I dozed the endless hours away, always thinking: another five, another four, another three, another two, just another hour, then we can see the sky again, breathe again.

The pumps would start up. A wonderful noise, relief, for we knew we had only a few more minutes to endure and pulled ourselves together to get through them. Surface! Hatch open! Fresh air would flood down into the boat as I scrambled clear. I breathed long, long and deep, as if for the first time in this world!

When surfacing was fully completed, the crew came up one by one. Each man had to make a brief pause in the hatch as he came off the tower ladder and I gave each face a searching look. I was appalled at what I saw. Pale green, dirty, unshaven faces, eyes red-ringed, a listless posture. But none would admit how he truly felt. There was no complaint, no murmur of protest, and they used this composure to convey the impression of strength. But their eyes said it all.

Actually I had an ulterior motive: I was weighing each man up because I had conceived an audacious plan. While we were below I had remembered our locker full of revolvers. Once it was clear that we could no longer escape from the English Channel in our submarine, we would have to resort to desperate measures. We would come up alongside a British armed trawler by night and capture it. It would mean handfighting with man pitted against man, but two things would be in our favour: the element of surprise and the fact that our men would go aboard already armed.

"Coxswain", I said to Becker when we were alone, "sometimes I think we ought to capture one of those English patrol vessels and use it to tow the boat to Zeebrugge." Becker gave me a grave look. He was no friend of schemes like these. "It could be done, Herr Oberleutnant," he said. No more was spoken on the subject, but it continued to occupy my thinking, as I had the ultimate responsibility for boat and crew. Certainly I believed that we would reach the nets at Calais, and that we would get through the Gap. But once beyond the nets, with our batteries drained, how would we fare then? The tidal stream set away from the Flanders coast. If we continued to drift, we would drift out into the North Sea, into the minefields of the North Sea.

The more I thought about the idea and assessed the men, the more I doubted the feasibility of the plan. What type of fight could I expect a starving, thirst-crazed crew to put up against the well-fed, fit hands manning a Royal Navy armed trawler? This was the weak point in the whole idea, but possibly it could be done if we were desperate enough.

Meanwhile persistent rumours had been issuing from the engine-room, where artificer Hausmann and his three helpers had been labouring day and night on the temporary coupling. Rarely did they cease from their hammering, jangling and filing, and then only for technical discussions. One noble idea kept them upright, drove them back time and again to their work on the coupling – the idea that they would save boat and crew if they succeeded.

Early on the fourth day Hausmann reported to me with a smile, "The coupling is ready. We can try it immediately."

The engine started up and ran for a few seconds before a dull thud announced failure. The engine died. The boat shuddered. We all knew what that meant: the coupling had sheared again. Nobody spoke or gestured. In a phlegmatic tone, the Coxswain remarked, "Such a short performance for so much work." It was not a criticism but there was no response. We all felt that with this failure our situation had deteriorated. Hausmann and Döring went back to work. Perhaps even they no longer believed it could be done, but that wouldn't stop them from continuing to try.

We were still surfaced; from a sunsight we knew that we had advanced, which was the important thing. The ordeal beneath the waves seemed worse than ever, but now we felt there was a purpose to it all. Six more hours down; late in the afternoon, when we returned to life, it was noticeably cooler and a little misty. The hours passed quickly. Shortly after dark we were due to submerge again. On making a last visual check I noticed in the far distance a string of twinkling lights. Could we have come as far as this? There was no doubt about it: we had Boulogne fine on the starboard bow.

The next six hours below were easier to suffer. The bodily agonies receded as we contemplated the imminent objective and the expectation of what the morrow would bring.

UB-2 surfaced at 0400 into a thick fog. Until now we had always been dogged by clear weather, but this fog was really a mixed blessing. I was relying on a land bearings for inshore navigation. On the other hand I could remain on the surface despite the heavy naval traffic and shipping, drifting along without using our precious batteries, conserving the power for the passage of Haecker's Gap.

I decided to allow the current to bear us through the fog towards Boulogne. As a precaution I flooded down so that the entire boat was under water except for the top 75 cms of the conning tower. The coxswain and I perched ourselves on the rim of the open bridge hatch keeping a sharp lookout. Could other vessels see us? In the fog they would most likely take us for a small fishing boat, certainly not a U-boat. In any case, it would take just ten seconds to submerge completely if surprised. Steamers and armed trawlers slid past us in the veils of mist. Long before we saw them we heard the steady thumping of their machinery across the oily sea.

By now it was 1000 hrs. Soon the current would reverse,

forcing us to submerge just short of Boulogne. It was necessary, but a hard decision to take. The problem was aggravated by our having to settle on a much deeper bottom than that frequented hitherto. This had its dangers. Our small U-boat had not been tested under pressure. Commanders were advised that dives below thirty to forty metres should be avoided. Thus a small uncertainty as to whether the boat could withstand the water pressure preceded the larger one, whether she could get through the Gap.

UB-2 reached forty metres quickly, then went deeper metre by metre. At fifty metres I had the boat trimmed and ordered the damage centres to report. There were no leakages. The dive continued. When the depth gauge indicated sixty metres I was biting my lip. Had we found the deepest hole here? At sixty-three metres we grounded with a crunch. Damn! Rocky ground. This was bad enough, but at this pressure it needed only a couple of rivets in the pressure hull to fail and we were done for. There was no time to dwell on this possibility, however, for the counter-current had set in and started to drag at the boat. She rolled first to this side, then to that, bumping continually against the rocky bottom. Steadily it grew more frequent and violent. A series of blows like a steam-hammer smashed against the hull as the current forced the boat remorselessly before it. Men sprang to their feet in alarm, their large eyes staring into the control room. Helplessly, they looked at artificer Hausmann and myself, who stood by the depth gauge and compressed air taps, ready to end the dive and surface should the danger become too great. To surface now, in the counter-current, would mean using electric power. We might as well give up our hopes of forcing the Gap! Logic said, Surface! The heart said, Remain down! We wouldn't surface yet, not until it was impossible to hold out, as long as our nerves and the boat could take it.

My gaze never strayed from the depth gauge. With a grumble and a thunderous roar the current raised the submarine from sixty-three to fifty-five metres, then rolled her on her beam. There was a crash, and a jolt reverberated through the boat, throwing us from our feet. Hausmann reached for the compressed air valve to blow the tanks. I grasped his arm. No! Another second! Wait! Courage! Slowly our brave little boat rolled upright as the depth gauge indicated fifty-seven metres. This explained the shaking up. As we were rolled across the rocks we had fallen a metre.

Finally, after ninety minutes, the current passed its peak and slackened and the boat settled, the blows became less violent. I looked at Hausmann. We were both bathed in sweat from the struggle and the fight for breath, gasping as if we had just completed a fast marathon.

We lay exhausted in our bunks, conserving our energies for what came next. Two hours more: one hour, ten minutes: the counter-flow ceased. We were before the Gap in daylight. The attempt would have to be made submerged using the periscope to navigate. The moment long dreamed of had arrived.

I brought the boat to periscope depth. Woe betide us if it was still foggy, for then it would have to be postponed. Another six hours of potash horror!

The head of the instrument broke surface. It was clear and sunny. I could see the coast of Boulogne. Becker took down three bearings on shore targets, fixed our position and gave me a course to steer for the Gap. This flood would set us north of Calais. While I was making the calculations, a patrol vessel came close and I retracted the periscope. A little later when I raised it again I held my breath in horror for a second, then bawled down into the control room, "Rudder hard to port, maximum revolutions, everything you've got!" I did not enlighten them as to the nature of the problem, since it would only cause disquiet. Cold sweat ran down my back at what I was seeing through the periscope. 500 metres ahead, blocking our line of drift as far as the French shore, stretched endless netting supported by gigantic buoys. This was a net we knew nothing about. As far as I knew, the main great net began seaward of the Gap and stretched to Dover. What we did not know was that immediately in front of the Gap a second heavy fence had been laid to the French shore and the current was drifting us straight into it. The tidal stream was making so strongly that although I had now turned the boat in a half-circle

29

to meet it with the electric motor full out, it was being slowly carried sternwards towards the net. Once our steering gear and propeller tangled in the meshes we were done for!

The boat drifted towards the trammel; our fate seemed sealed. Suddenly I noticed that my view of the last buoy at the seaward end of the net, which lay about 200 metres to port, had been blocked by the naval trawler. I put the boat at an oblique angle across the stream so that while she was bearing down on the net the sheer was taking her towards the outer buoy. It was now a race between the tidal stream and the sheer. If the stream won, it was curtains for *UB-2*.

I had to restrict my periscope observations to quick peeps because of the proximity of the enemy vessel. We seemed to be closing the net too fast! I saw the wash foaming around the buoys as they interrupted the tidal flow, watched with bated breath as we came nearer and nearer. It was touch and go. Now we ran towards the great surface hawser supporting the net; only a few more seconds to disaster, and then – the enormous outer buoy passed ten metres away on my starboard hand.

Dripping with sweat I stood at the periscope, utterly exhausted. I called down for a supplementary cup of our rationed water to celebrate my success, which had been all due to fast reactions. The water refreshed me. Not once now did my gaze stray from the optic. There must be no more surprises if we were to be off Calais by nightfall. But everything went to plan. After a short while we passed through the gap which Haecker had reconnoitred. That evening, before the eastwards current alternated, we surfaced for fresh air. In the distance glittered the lights of Calais. We were through.

How often we had dreamed of this moment in the dark, grim hours of the last few days!

Soon the powerful counter-current set in again and we were forced to take the bottom, but this time the ground here was soft sand, and this swishing and rustling was much easier on the ear than what we had gone through the previous night off Boulogne. Towards five the next morning we surfaced and let the tidal stream drift us eastwards. It was now time to contact the U-Flotilla. The telegraphist morsed the radio station of the Naval Corps Flanders. No reply. If they couldn't hear us, then who would come to our aid?

I had decided there would be no further six-hour periods on the bottom. We had had more than we could stomach of it. When the current turned, we merely anchored. It was not so dangerous to do so in this area, as enemy naval units rarely frequented it. Actually we did spot a French torpedo-boat passing in the distance, but I remained surfaced. The warship, which was heading at high speed for Calais, showed no interest in us. Who knew what more important task awaited him there?

After the stream turned we drifted eastwards. Our telegraphist, Schepp, called up the Naval Corps radio stations repeatedly but received no response. For some time we had not been receiving Norddeich which included Army bulletins. This was a little unsettling, for we had no means of knowing whether there might not be problems at the Front. However, the humidity in the boat had been very high and I assumed this had adversely affected the boat's telegraphy installation. It was very urgent for me to restore contact with our forces, for we were in desperate need of assistance. The current was forcing the boat north-east in the direction of the Dutch coast and we were bearing down on the British-laid minefields. Some way in the distance the first perimeter marker had been seen from the bridge.

Hausmann and Meyer had continued to toil undespairingly at the broken coupling. They were optimistic and thought a test would be possible by the evening: I spent a great deal of time in the engine-room to give them encouragement.

Towards 2030 hrs the coxswain reported down, "Herr Oberleutnant, I just saw briefly a submarine surface astern. He dived immediately, distance four sea miles." I scrambled up to the bridge. That was all we needed, after all our valiant sacrifices, to be knocked off by a British submarine on the doorstep. I decided that we should shelter in the minefield. We had just enough juice in the batteries to crawl inside. Once behind the first barrier the batteries would be completely drained, but at least we would be safe from the British. Nobody liked to stalk the enemy through his own minefields. At slow speed we slipped between two fat mines wallowing half out of the water. We looked, but were unable to spot others undoubtedly lurking just below the surface. Once we had given the two mines ample clearance I had the motor stopped. I went down into the engine-room to see how the work on the coupling was progressing. An hour passed.

Suddenly the alarm bell rang. I sprinted to the control centre. The coxswain shouted to me, "Dive immediately. Submarine surfaced very close by!" Using only three rungs of the ladder on my way up to the bridge I saw the submarine at once and yelled down, "Don't flood! Don't flood!" gasping like a whale. A U-boat was surfacing about 30 metres away. I saw the stare of its two great eyes and the leering shark's mouth. The hatch-lid of the other boat was thrown open, a cap waved and tiny Oberleutnant Hans Valentiner shouted over, "I say, Fips, you were lucky there! I had you down for English. My torpedoes were ready. I was just about to push the button and then, at the very last moment, I saw your gorgeous eyes! They're your lucky talisman. Shame about my English submarine though!"

It transpired that our considerate Flotilla CO had sent Valentiner out to look for us. Now Hänschen would bear us home in triumph. But we had our pride too. First we would try out our repair to the coupling. Fifteen minutes later we were ready; the engine was thrown into gear: the boat gave a jolt. So it wasn't to be. I offered Hausmann my hand.

Quickly, Valentiner passed us his hawser and towed us through the dazzlingly lit night sea to Ostend. We arrived next morning. I phoned Flotilla CO Bartenbach in Bruges, and he could not believe he was hearing my voice. He had long given us up for lost. I learnt that the other three Channel boats had all returned home without making a kill; this gave us a certain degree of consolation.

Our game little *UB-2* was to provide more sterling services to the Flanders U-Flotilla, but never again did she test the waters of the Channel. We were to share many future experiences with Hänschen Valentiner and his crew, and bonded with them in true comradeship, but eventually the inexorable wheels of war ground them under.

Chapter 2

AN UNPLEASANT SURPRISE
ON THE ENGLISH COAST

The operational mission of *UB-2* to Le Havre was neither a military success nor strictly a feat of sporting endurance. It was more a life and death struggle to get the boat home and ourselves with it. That had been the true value of the mission, for the shared experience of the terrible strain and danger had bonded the crew and so laid the foundation for all our later successes.

UB-2 required only a short lay-up in dock. The coupling was repaired and replacements were found for the five crewmen who had had to be put ashore with a heart condition following the voyage. *UB-2* was ready to sail again.

The next operation took us to the English coast off Lowestoft. This was a sector where U-boats mainly kept an eye out for enemy warships since we could only attack merchant shipping under prescribed conditions which were highly unfavourable for us.

It was the second day of the mission. During the day I cruised underwater inshore along a section of the English coast. British destroyers were observed in the distance and I gave ample sea room to a pair of armed naval trawlers patrolling up and down. However, by the time darkness fell no worthwhile opportunity for attack had presented itself. The long period submerged had almost drained the battery and without electric power I would not be able to carry out a night attack. Therefore late that afternoon I headed offshore and for the purpose of recharging picked a spot where I thought we could remain on the surface undisturbed.

It was a starry night, dark and warm. There was no wind and the sea was black and smooth as silk. Occasionally a wave slapped against the hull. Far to the west a few lights twinkled on the coast. If anybody spoke it seemed his voice must carry miles across the water. The recharging of the battery was an essential job but involved running the diesel and the ventilation machinery at the same time. The racket was appalling. The noise was so loud in the dangerous quiet that the longer it went on the less comfortable I felt about it. I was mindful of the two patrol boats we had steered clear of earlier in the day. If they heard us, it would alert them to our presence, something I was most keen to avoid since I was determined to nail at least one of them that very night in a surface attack. On the surface the boat had a certain prospect of success even if the patrol vessel made a fortuitous change of course while the attack was being prepared.

When I was informed, in resposnse to my enquiry after the recharging had been going on for two hours, that the battery was not yet near a full charge, I had the operation stopped – a great relief to the ears – and crept slowly back under water towards the coast. After some time we were close to the position where the two armed trawlers had been charted earlier in the day. I stopped and lay in wait. I wanted to see if anything worthwhile was about. We were a little south of Lowestoft, about three miles offshore.

Adrift, it seemed there was an exciting stillness over the waters. Wherever one peered into the blackness, dark shadows were moving silently. Again and again one would raise the binoculars to the eyes and find nothing there. The absence of the normal yardstick by which distance was estimated deceived the senses. The horizon was invisible and the sea surface as seen through the glasses shimmered everywhere indistinguishably. A spot of sea could as easily be two hundred metres away as two thousand. We were oppressed by the fear that at any moment an anti-submarine vessel might suddenly sneak up on us, perhaps under a grey sail. All of us perched on the tower, the coxswain, the two lookouts and I, had this presentiment.

In the distance the dull thump of a ship's machinery gradually became audible. I hoped this would be one of the two naval vessels. Since we were all unhappy about the various tricks our eyes had played on us in the darkness, I had the boat flooded down. The dive tanks were trimmed so that only the top third of the three-metre-high conning tower projected above the surface of the sea. This gave us the security of knowing that we would definitely see an approaching vessel before he saw us, and the boat could be submerged within only a few seconds. This made us feel much safer.

We waited and waited. The distant noise was unceasing. Suddenly I had the impression that the night had grown darker without at first being able to account for it exactly. Then I noticed that all the little pinpoints of light twinkling on the coast had been dowsed. Now we were in absolute darkness. Why had the British suddenly extinguished their coastal lighting? Was this a black-out for a Zeppelin attack? The sound of the ship's machinery had also ceased, and now *UB-2* wallowed silently in the leaden black sea. We spent the next three-quarters of an hour waiting and listening. Suddenly there began a distant humming. First one man heard it, then all could. It grew louder gradually. These would be our Zeppelins! The humming assumed a steady pitch, distant but perfectly clear. Suddenly we were startled as the whole coast lit up and ten to twenty searchlights criss-crossed the starry heavens with probing fingers of brilliant light. A magical scene. At sea level the illumination provided by the beams revealed a deserted coastal strip. After five minutes, as abruptly as they had appeared, the great confusion of rays vanished and darkness enveloped the sea once more. The humming could still be heard but what made it had trespassed onwards into the night. What next?

The dull thump of a ship's screw started up again, louder than before. We stared hard into the night – and saw a shadow. It was one of the naval patrol vessels, heading south but out of torpedo range and steaming so fast that we had no hope of catching him. I would have to stay put and hope that he returned on a parallel course. After all, to patrol up and down was evidently the main reason for his existence.

Within half an hour two things happened at once: a second naval trawler made an appearance following the track of the first but a little more to seaward while the first was now seen bearing down on us from the south. Quickly I had the torpedo tube readied. The line of approach to us looked just right and all I had to do was open the angle a little without shifting from our position. When everything was ready I observed from the geometry that he would be quite close when the torpedo was fired. I could also appreciate how good the visibility actually was now that I had a firm objective in view, both being matters which caused me some disquiet, although I could do nothing about either. Being flooded down the boat was virtually un-manoeuvrable and I had no time to draw back.

The black shadow of the naval trawler was pounding up fast, his outline increasingly distinct as he emerged from the darkness. "All hands to diving stations!" I ordered. At the word of command we could be completely below the surface within ten seconds. The coxswain and I sat on the rim of the bridge hatch in a fever of excitement, the situation growing more tense by the moment. We dared not even whisper. I picked out details on the enemy fo'c'sle – two lookouts forward, and a cannon. Already they would have seen us, but probably have taken us for a rowing boat. Reluctantly the coxswain and I bent forward to reduce our own outline. I had the word "Flood!" on my lips, for the moment would soon arrive when he recognized us for what we were and turned to ram.

Suddenly a lamp was turned on at the level of his wheelhouse and a message blinked out. He had not yet concluded that we were hostile. I had no time to read off what he was asking as I was more interested in whether he would keep to his present course or turn towards us. The lamp ceased its chatter, inviting us to reply. When we failed to do so, the question was repeated. We remained immobile, gritting our teeth, waiting for the firing angle to arrive.

The situation was damn ticklish. The nearer he came to the firing angle, the better were his chances to destroy us should he decide to attack. If he recognized us now as a U-boat, it was doubtful that we could escape his ramming manoeuvre. It was dicey, but I wouldn't give in. I sent the coxswain down into the tower and sat alone on the rim of the hatch, my hand grasping the lid, ready to pull it shut behind me should the evil moment present itself! I was swearing softly, daring to make only the briefest glances at the patrol vessel which was now so close that I could make out every detail. Surely he must be able to see me as clearly as I saw him? The seconds ticked away, an eternity. He had failed to recognize us as a U-boat. He had missed his chance. Within a few seconds I would fire.

I straightened, stood up, checked the firing data, took aim and shouted below, "*Achtung! Los!*"

A push of a button and the torpedo set off for the target. A few seconds later a jolt shook the boat and almost simultaneously a gigantic explosive column spouted up at the stern of the patrol vessel. A shout of jubilation resounded below. As if spellbound I stared at the sinking wreck. Meanwhile the coxswain had returned to the bridge and called out, "Second patrol boat coming straight for us!" Within a few seconds *UB-2* had slipped into the safety of the depths.

The events of the night preyed on my mind and I sought sleep in vain. It was late the next morning before I brought the boat to periscope depth for a surface observation. We were alone. I took the boat out to sea and surfaced in patchy mist to recharge the battery. A sharp watch was maintained. The operation had been in hand for about three hours when a shadow was reported six points to starboard. All binoculars focused on the indistinct shape in the drifting veils of fog.

"Looks like a sailing boat," the boatswain muttered.

Slowly two large sails became evident, and then the hull completed the picture. I allowed the recharging to proceed calmly. This one wouldn't outrun us so easily. Half an hour later we had topped up the battery and set off after the quarry. The wind was slack and he had made very little progress meanwhile.

As we were coming up on the ketch, I thought about *UB-4*. The boat was supposed to be operating off the Hoofden and had not been heard from for two months. In Bruges they thought *UB-4* had been the victim of a British Q-ship, a disguised anti-submarine vessel. Whether or not that was likely, I decided that in this case, at any rate, I would accord this particular bird some respect.

A gentle breeze had sprung up from the north. The ketch continued at no great speed towards Lowestoft. I came well forward of his course and turned to bring him fine on the bow before closing in.

I sent the men to diving stations and ordered the machine gun set up on the bridge. The coxswain and the gunner, Schlör, were alone with me on the tower. At 500 metres I had a burst of fire sprayed across his track. There was no reaction aboard the tub.

"Coxswain, do you think the beefeaters didn't hear that?"

"Herr Oberleutnant, they must have heard it. This all looks very fishy to me."

"Then I think we will have to show a bit of caution here. Schlör, bounce a few peas across his deck."

Four or five single rounds spattered the planks of the ketch, but still nothing stirred.

At the wheel in the stern stood an ancient mariner, a shag pipe clenched between his teeth, his body half-turned away so as to keep us on his blind side. At 300 metres I favoured this old salt with a long stare through my binoculars. "That helmsman is either stone deaf or he's got nerves of steel," I said. No sooner had I completed the sentence than four or five men sprang nimbly on deck from a cabin midships and threw down a lean-to to expose a deck-cannon at us. At once I gave Schlör the order for rapid fire. He got off two rounds before there was an awful silence, some fumbling with the weapon and then he reported in a subdued voice that the gun had jammed. Well of course it would jam, right now when we really needed it!

Meanwhile the ketch had fired and the three of us ducked involuntarily as the first shell howled overhead. The second dropped fifteen metres short. Schlör exclaimed, "MG is clear!" But they had straddled us; the next round would hit! It was time to go. "Flood!" I screamed, rang down for full ahead, put the rudder hard over, thrust Becker and Schlör through the bridge hatch and followed them. As I pulled the hatch cover shut I saw the third shell throw up a huge column of water close alongside. My heart was in my mouth as the boat dived; a hit now would sink us for sure.

The smart turning manoeuvre and crash dive was our salvation: they couldn't touch us submerged.

"That was a close shave," Becker remarked as the depth gauge indicated ten metres.

"Something to tell my brothers about," I replied with a gnash of the teeth.

The engineer trimmed the boat at twenty metres and I set off for the coast at top speed. After his tangle with us, the ketch would now have escape as his priority; this lay among his own patrol vessels on the coast. He knew that we would not be prepared merely to disengage just like that; there was an account to be settled. Before he got to safety he had to be sunk with the last torpedo.

This was not likely to be easy. A ketch has no great draught and the torpedo would have to be set to run shallow; shallow-set torpedoes tended to be irregular at keeping to the required depth. Nevertheless, he would have a souvenir, and I was prepared to sacrifice my last eel regardless. The crew had been put in the picture by Schlör, who had naturally recounted the recent events in close detail.

My calculations showed that we would arrive in a favourable position for the attack within twenty minutes. At the end of this period, I reduced speed and cautiously ascended to periscope depth. It was a tense moment. Would he be there?

Through the optic I saw at first only green water, then the tip of the periscope broke the surface again and again permitting me to snatch the briefest looks around. There was no sign of the quarry. I raised the periscope glass completely above the wave-tops and saw our friend approaching from exactly the spot I had expected to see him. "Boys, boys, now we'll give him what for," I said.

Carefully I steered the boat round to a shooting position. The ketch was very close and I had to be careful not to expose the periscope head for more than a few seconds at a time. I was seized by the fever of the hunt. We were coming nearer. Along his decks he had posted a number of lookouts who were now scouring the wave-tops. Pray they don't spot us! I called down to the engineer to keep the depth absolutely precisely. The least variation could expose the periscope to the ketch and ruin everything. A few more seconds remained until I would fire. With all the raising and lowering of the periscope, I was almost breathless going up and down the conning tower ladder. "*Achtung*!" I stretched the final word of command into two long syllables, raised the periscope, saw the target exactly in the cross-wires and shouted "*Los!*"

The boat gave a shrug, the sign that a torpedo had been discharged. This was the trickiest moment for the engineer, to keep the boat trimmed at the correct depth following the sudden expulsion of the heavy missile. The tendency was for the bows to rise with a kick like a mule. At a hand signal all hands rushed forward and restored the trim with their combined weight. Meanwhile I had retracted the periscope so that nothing should betray the attack before the torpedo hit.

The coxswain had started a stop-watch. "What is the range, Herr Oberleutnant?"

"About three hundred metres."

"Then the torpedo should hit after twenty seconds." Sure enough, after twenty seconds there was a huge explosion which rocked the boat. "Hurrah!" shouted the crew.

"Blow all tanks!" I would surface at once to inspect the plight of the Q-ship. The boat popped up like a cork. As soon as the tower protruded a metre above the surface, I threw open the hatch cover, jumped out and stared – aghast! The ketch was just passing at about 300-metres off the beam as if nothing had happened. As soon as he spotted us, he trained his deck gun and the first round fell just short of midships, giving me a shower as the water spout collapsed over the bridge. I dived through the hatch shouting "Flood! Full ahead!" and we crash-dived to safety.

I held a conference with the coxswain and chief engineer. The shallow-set torpedo had evidently hit the bottom and gone off there, which accounted for the force of the explosion. What more could we do to get this ketch? Nothing. In our haste to get below the machine gun had been left on the bridge and the seawater ruined it. In abject misery I gave the order to head for home.

We had at least established the probable fate of *UB-4* and her crew.* We would have gone the same way if we had not got under so smartly. On meeting outwardly civilian vessels we would have to keep our distance in future. The British liked sport, in which gunnery was included. We were quite happy to join in and play by the rules, but we really preferred to know in advance if the other fellow was toting a gun!

---

* *UB-4* (Oberleutnant Karl Gross) was surprised and sunk off Smith's Knoll buoy by the armed fishing smack *Inverlyon* on 15 August 1915.

Chapter 3

FRIENDS IN THE AIR

The encounter with a disguised naval anti-submarine vessel masquerading as a ketch was a salutary lesson for us. This and other experiences had taught us that our small U-boats were too weakly armed to hold their own against a British fishing smack with a deck-gun. The Flotilla Chief had accordingly issued a standing instruction that sailing vessels should be tackled by two U-boats working as a pair.

My friend Hans Valentiner and I were given a joint operation of this nature in August 1915. Our two boats set out from Bruges together for Zeebrugge, where we were held in thick fog for hours. We rejoiced when at last it lifted and allowed us to put to sea and away from the dangers on the coast, not least of which were the "refreshments" obtained from the "Pope of the Mole", the most seaward coastal artillery installation of the Western Front.

It gave us an oddly secure feeling to sail out as a pair. Of course, it took us a while to discover the most practical manner of proceeding and how best to react in the eventuality of being forced to dive by the enemy. On a number of occasions British destroyers were sighted, unfortunately not within striking distance. We both dived, and although remaining submerged for several hours re-established contact without difficulty.

Late on the afternoon of the second day we were about thirty sea miles off Lowestoft. A light westerly breeze was ruffling the sea, the sun was hidden by a low mist. Valentiner was at about three hundred metres in line astern. I was on the tower and, glancing aft on one occasion, I saw his signaller flagging to me "Zeppelins starboard quarter".

Necks craned to look; then we spotted them, three great airships, their long round bodies partially obscured as they droned majestically nearer at high speed through the cloud and mist. Gradually they become wholly visible. They ranged over a variety of altitudes, sometimes for a short time beneath the cloud cover, then they would rise up into it and disappear from sight for minutes at a time. I hoped they had seen and recognized us! The Zeppelins were cruising at between five and six hundred metres, but from that altitude the two U-boats far below would be no more than two specks and we might easily be overlooked, which was a cause of some concern to us.

We had fired off our recognition flares much too early and waited anxiously for a reply, which failed to come. Ever nearer they bumbled, materializing from the mists like three fantastic grey monsters of some fabulous myth. If we had not known these for our own German airships we would be quaking at the knees by now.

One recognition flare after another soared towards them. It was essential that they responded. They were no more than five hundred metres astern, the roar of their engines was deafening – and still they hadn't deigned to acknowledge our signal. Suddenly the middle Zeppelin seemed to notice us, dipped his nose – and opened fire! He had mistaken us for British! I glanced astern and saw that Hans Valentiner was diving fast. Within a trice I followed suit.

The hands who had been on the bridge tumbled all ends up into the tower. Cursing, I plummeted down after them. If his aim was any good we were lost! Nobody timed it but I am certain that this was the fastest dive UB-2 ever made. All dive valves were thrown open and the boat was soon so heavy that she sank out of control to the bottom and hit the sea bed with a spine-jarring thump. Nevertheless I breathed a sigh of relief. I was just beginning to recover my composure when a bomb went off very close by with the most tremendous explosion.

The coxswain looked at me with a grin. "Bombing like that makes you really proud of our German airmen, doesn't it?" Well might he laugh, but I didn't find it at all amusing; another one like that a little bit nearer and it was curtains. Fortunately nothing else came down and shortly afterwards I judged it safe to venture back to the surface. The dirigibles had droned off on their mission over England. There were obviously more important things to do than plaster their own U-boats.

UB-2 had the sea to herself; there was no sign of Hänschen Valentiner. Apparently he had more respect for our Zeppelins than I did. It was another ten minutes before he reappeared and we laid our boats almost alongside for a chat.

We agreed it had been a rum affair, for while they had either not seen or ignored our signal flares, they had not demanded the recognition signal before attacking. This was a matter for the Admiral Staff!

"Did you get their numbers?" I asked Valentiner.

"Definitely. I made a point of getting the number of the middle one, the one which dropped the bomb. It was number thirty-five."

Well this was a fine affair. It had been my own uncle, Herbert Ehrlich, commander of Z-35, who had tried to kill his own nephew! Well then, he would have to make up for it by digging deep into his wallet at the officers' club!

As we were later able to confirm, the Zeppelins had simply not seen our flares. Our submarines were of a type not seen in the German Bight where our airships spent most of their time in scouting operations, and it never occurred to them that we could be anything other than enemy. From now on we would have to exercise a degree of caution in the face of even friendly air forces.

It was six months later before Valentiner and I caught up with my uncle, by which time he and I had effected a reconciliation. Nevertheless, as recompense for the heavy sample he had dropped on us from his perch on high that day he willingly footed an extremely heavy bill from the wine cellar of the officers' club.

Chapter 4

COMMERCE WARFARE IN ACCORDANCE WITH THE PRIZE REGULATIONS

In April 1916 I was given a new boat, *UB-39*. Built at Blohm & Voss, Hamburg, she was an improved version of *UB-2*, being twice the size and equipped with two diesel engines instead of one, which provided a radius of action three times greater. For surface attacks the machine gun had been augmented by an 8.8-cm rapid-fire deck gun. I managed to arrange for the majority of the crew of the *UB-2* to transfer to the new boat with me and this was our great strength.

Contrary to my previous experiences, a voyage in *UB-39* was straightforward and safe. We brought the boat from Kiel to Zeebrugge with ease, and with my new command I enjoyed a period of stimulating and successful distant water operations. I was thankful to be rid of the monotonous sentry duties adrift off the Belgian coast which now fell to the new, younger commanders taking over our old boats as their first commands.

Germany was still pursuing warfare against merchant shipping in accordance with the Prize Regulations which provided that no hostile action could be taken against an enemy or neutral ship until she had been stopped and her documents examined for evidence of contraband.

On one of these voyages with the new boat along the English

east coast I arrived off the small Durham coastal town of Seaham. There was a westerly wind, and clouds of thick white smoke were belching out over the sea from the direction of the harbour. A quick glance at the chart told me that the source of the smoke would be a large iron foundry that lay on high ground just south of the town. This would undoubtedly be producing munitions!

Planning a follow-up operation upon my return I requested permission from my Flotilla Chief to bombard the Seaham ironworks. This was granted, but Bartenbach urged the greatest caution since in his opinion the town was bound to be defended by coastal batteries.

I went home on leave to my mother at Harzburg, to find a house visited by grief. Shortly after Christmas 1914 when I was watch officer on Schwieger's *U-20*, the boat had put into the naval repair yard at Ostend to repair a damaged diesel. Our arrival there had caused great excitement. The town of Ostend, which was being used as a rest centre for German troops after the heavy fighting, was swarming with army personnel of all ranks, many of whom now poured down into the interior of *U-20*. Schwieger improvised a sightseeing tour of the boat which resulted in literally hundreds of visitors in field-grey crawling through the pressure hull. He considered this to be an obligation, even though it put a strain on the crew.

One day while I was sitting in the commander's cabin with Schwieger and the Chief Engineer there was a knock at the door and a dishevelled rifleman entered, covered in mud from head to toe, asking to speak to Oberleutnant Fürbringer. I gave the scruff a look and then embraced him. It was my second eldest brother, a man who liked to paint, a private in an infantry regiment. Entering Ostend fresh from the trenches, he had happened to glimpse a U-boat and just knew it must be mine. The poor fellow had suffered very much. At Ypres he had been wounded in the hand. As an artist this was a terrible blow, so we gave him a couple of large swigs of rum to compensate him for it.

He accepted my invitation to dine at the officers' club that evening, and I succeeded in reviving his spirits. While there I happened to run into his Company Commander who expressed satisfaction with my brother's performance at the Front and promised to try to help him. We had a few more happy days together in Ostend as the diesel repair took longer than expected. It was the last time that I was able to enjoy the company of my dear, dear brother. Twice more he was wounded and then could outrun his fate no longer. In heroic foreknowledge of the inevitable, he fell on 31 May 1916, the day of the Battle of Jutland, at point Dead Man outside the fortress of Verdun.

After fourteen days' leave I set out for Seaham. On the afternoon of my arrival in the operational area I went inshore and took periscope bearings on various prominent marks inland. There was a favourable westerly wind and I decided to attack at dusk. I selected the spot from where I would make the bombardment and settled the boat down on the sea bed there.

I considered dusk to be the best time for the attack because the boat would be difficult to locate against the backdrop of night and, provided it persisted, the westerly wind would drift the smoke from the iron foundry chimney over the inshore waters. Furthermore I was assuming that the factory would have only a skeleton staff on the premises at night: my objective was the destruction of war materials and not people.

The bombardment would not be without its risks. British naval vessels were constantly patrolling in the neighbourhood. If any were off Seaham at the wrong time, the attack would have to be postponed. In a state of high excitement we began our preparations to surface at 2030 hrs. The shells were fused and the gun crew painted humorous messages on them. We had one hundred 8.8-cm rounds on board but we could hardly fire off the whole magazine as a reserve was required for possible use in the commerce war at sea. The gun crew suggested that *UB-39* should fire a symbolic thirty-nine rounds. I agreed. It was actually fewer than I was proposing but the range was so short that every shell was bound to hit the target and thirty-nine shells was probably enough to demolish the foundry completely.

48

Shortly after 2100 hrs I came to periscope depth. As I expected it was already dusk. A light westerly wind was wafting layers of white smoke low down over the area to seaward from where I would conduct the bombardment. We were so close in that it also partially obscured my view of the factory, so I brought the boat to another position from where I had a good view of the factory installations. Very close to the ironworks I saw the small town of Seaham.

Several small naval vessels were cruising to the north and south of my position and in addition there was a destroyer to the north steaming out to sea at full speed. On account of the unfavourable conditions, I felt sure that none of these vessels, nor the coastal batteries, would be able to see the boat, and even if they could, the attack would be over and done with before they fully realized what had happened.

Once I was satisfied with my position I gave the order to blow tanks. The boat surfaced quickly. At the word of command the gun crew poured out of the tower and sprinted down the forecasing to clear the deck gun. A few seconds later officer of the watch Leutnant Busse reported the gun ready to fire. I gave the order "Rapid fire!" and a succession of shells barked out from the barrel. Our fire was accurate, hit after hit on the ironworks! Before the naval trawlers or coastal batteries had come to their senses we had fired all thirty-nine and the watch officer reported, "Bombardment completed!" This was excellent. We were still undisturbed; perhaps they were still reeling under the thunder. As I drew off the coast I saw the naval vessels and the destroyer all converging on Seaham, smoke pouring from their stacks. This could get unpleasant. I dived to thirty metres and stole away from the scene.

Next morning we embarked on our commerce war in earnest. Despite the difficulties, our boat quickly sank fourteen steam trawlers, as well as a number of smaller craft. I recognize that these seafarers were a special breed, always ready to return to sea aboard a new fishing vessel after having had the previous boat sunk beneath them. Such sinkings were not an enjoyable experience for them, for if they were sunk in bad weather the U-boat would not be prepared to spend time ensuring that the lifeboat reached the coast safely, and they knew that. I also admired the humour of these English fishermen in their hard existence. I always treated them as well as I could when taking them aboard, and we often used to have chats seaman to seaman.

On one occasion after sinking a steam trawler I picked up her eight crewmen. One stepped forward from the group on the foredeck, gave my men a searching look and then demanded to be taken to the commander. I motioned for him to approach the conning tower and asked what he wanted, to which he adopted a semi-military bearing and shouted up, "I would like to inform you, sir, that this is my third time on your submarine, and I thank you for your good treatment."

"And I hope to see you many more times in the future," I responded with a beguiling gesture, at which the other fishermen all broke out in roars of laughter.

We headed for home several days later. Approaching the mole at Zeebrugge, a number of special preparations had to be made. At the seaward extremity of the mole was installed a coastal battery equipped with 8.8-cm rapid fire cannons under the command of Oberleutnant (Coastal Artillery Reserve) Schütte. His post was in fact the outermost artillery emplacement of the entire Western Front and by reason of his isolated existence at the end of the two-thousand-metre-long breakwater he was known universally as The Pope of the Mole. He was also the most decent fellow in the world.

Crewmen aboard U-boats putting to sea or returning were able to obtain from him all their requirements, including drink. Virtually every U-boat passing the mole would pull alongside the molehead to greet the Pope. I had done so when putting to sea on the present voyage, and a bet had been struck between us for a magnum of champagne that I would succeed in obtaining the bell from every vessel we sank. I had actually achieved this feat, *ergo* the special preparations. As proof of my success I hoisted on my ensign staff captured British and Dutch flags above the naval code flags for "Total of sixteen", corresponding to our tally for the voyage. Along the railings aft I rigged up eight ship's bells per side, two of them being particularly large specimens. The sixteen bells were attended by eight crewmen.

On the mole meanwhile my irregular flag signal had given rise to great excitement. As we approached a deafening peal of bells rang out at a prearranged word of command. The artillerymen responded joyfully with a cannibal dance. Using the exuberance of the occasion, I moored for a few minutes to claim my prize, and I was honoured by the appearance of the Pope himself, tears in his eyes and bearing the promised magnum. So emotional was the occasion that only with some difficulty could he be ushered off the boat.

After a patrol one was naturally in haste to get ashore in Bruges. The champagne was sufficient to quench the thirst of the three officers of *UB-39* during the passage of the Bruges canal and to engender a mood appropriate to the success of the voyage. Naturally we were keen to socialize with the folk of the mole but this was not the time.

Translator's Note

The *Durham Advertiser* of 14 July 1916 devoted a column of thirteen lines to an incident under a caption GERMAN SUBMARINE ATTACK ON SEAHAM in which it was stated that Seaham Harbour, an undefended small town on the coast of Durham, had been bombarded on the night of Tuesday 12 July 1916 by a German submarine, which fired at a few hundred yards' range about 30 shells from a 3-inch gun. The shells appeared to have fallen in the countryside beyond the town of Seaham towards Dalton-le-Dale and New Seaham, over two miles from the coast.

Fürbringer's account of the destruction of the Seaham iron foundry was a fabrication. The range was under half a mile and obviously he fired to miss, a fact he might have been a little uncomfortable in advertising to the German readership of his book. Local historians advance the theory that he knew the town from prewar and had a special affection for it, but Fürbringer had no connection with Seaham. The idea for the attack was his own. If he had been unhappy with the prevailing conditions, he could have offered any number of reasons for postponing or breaking off the bombardment. The point of pretending that the bombardment had successfully achieved its objective was to spare the Seaham iron foundry any future attentions.

His attack was to be mounted from south of the Outer Harbour. The water here is deep and affords a good view of the iron foundry from a range of about 600 yards. The factory is roughly triangular in shape with sides approximately 200 yards in length and surrounded by residential streets. The crucial moment occurred when he surfaced the boat prior to the attack and observed the target through binoculars: *Unmittelbar neben dem Eisenwerk sehe ich das kleine Städtchen Seaham* – "Very close to the iron foundry I saw the small town of Seaham." Fürbringer was under the impression that the iron foundry was a munitions factory. That was why he was attacking it. Suddenly he saw the close proximity of the town of Seaham and must have realized that if the munitions factory exploded, the town would also be destroyed. "My objective was the destruction of war materials and not people," he explained. Accordingly, on the grounds of the high risk to an enemy residential area, he deliberately fired long, a humanitarian decision by a very gallant officer. I am indebted to Ms Joan Weighell, Information Services Librarian, Durham City Reference Library, Mrs Lorna Wright, Senior Library Assistant, Seaham Library and Mr T McNee, the local historian, for providing information, cuttings and mapwork.

Chapter 5

WHERE IS LEUTNANT BUSSE?

We of the Flanders U-Flotilla had really gone for John Bull. The British knew all about us. Probably of all the German arms of service it was the U-boat arm which caused them the worst of their headaches and of these the Flanders boats gave them the most grief. From Bruges, Zeebrugge and Ostend we streamed out to attack Britain's lifeline in the English Channel; a U-boat Flotilla based on the Isle of Wight could have been only a morsel more troublesome than the weapon wielded by Bartenbach at Bruges.

If only we had been allowed to seize the initiative, if only we had not been always subject to an ever-increasing list of restrictions inflicted on us from above, which kept our success within such meagre limits. What exactly were they waiting for? Why were we not fully deployed? These were the questions always asked when we swapped experiences on convivial reunions in the officers' club after returning from our missions. But we were not so convivial when we remembered just how many of our comrades would never return.

Over fifty per cent of the German U-boat force was sunk, over eighty-three per cent of the Flanders U-boats. If there was a sharp edge to the war at sea, it was turned towards us.

When unrestricted U-boat warfare had still not been authorized by September 1916, our Flotilla Chief decided to mount an operation similar to that attempted a year previously, a simultaneous strike by four small U-boats off ports either side of the English Channel. On this occasion, however, he had at his disposal the far more efficient B-2 boats, including my own *UB-39*. The choice of operational area was left to the four commanders, and we agreed that we would operate wherever it appeared most favourable to the individual captain. It was decided to run the Straits between Dover and Calais at night because it was easier then to avoid the anti-submarine net barrage towed by enemy patrol vessels.

The four U-boats put out in fine weather and effected a rendezvous at British buoy 2501 about 12 sea miles north of Calais. I was considerably delayed en route by a minor engine problem and when I arrived I found the other three boats already moored one behind the other. We waited for dusk. About 1830 hrs all four boats streamed out westwards and contact was soon lost between us in the darkness. Passage through the endless row of British net boats, deep-sea steam trawlers each drifting at one end of a 100-metre-long anti-submarine net strung across our course, was no easy matter, as the line was constantly patrolled by British destroyers. We broke through in mid-Channel and continued westwards.

I set course for the western exit of the Channel where I felt confident of finding lively merchant traffic with a low degree of naval activity. Because of the British naval blockade elsewhere food was becoming scarce in Germany, and our glee can be imagined at the discovery of three thousand eggs aboard the first sinking of the patrol, the British steamer *Targus*. We could hardly find room for them in the boat. Over the next few days each man received twelve to fourteen eggs daily. Once our lust for them began to dwindle, the remainder were served up in a number of guises, coffee made with three or four whipped eggs being especially popular. Because of the heat in the boat, they could not be stored and it was left to the crew to use them up in the way they thought best.

The patrol was successful, although eventually the presence of enemy naval units forced me to operate further west, off the island of Ushant, where British and French forces were less of a hindrance.

Three days before the end of the patrol it became misty and I had to exercise more caution as the boat could be easily surprised in the conditions. At about midday a large freighter came lumbering up from the south-west, Norwegian colours painted on the ship's side indicated a claim to neutrality. I fired a shot across his bows and hoisted flag signals ordering the master to send his ship's papers across in a boat. My perusal of these soon established that this was the steamer *Pronto* carrying foodstuffs from Spain to Britain. This was contraband and the regulations allowed me to sink the ship. Next I hoisted signals ordering the vessel to be abandoned; the men were to proceed to the submarine in a lifeboat towing a second, empty lifeboat. Once these were both alongside, my prize crew of a Petty Officer and two men under Leutnant Busse crossed to the steamer in the second boat with explosive charges which would be used to scuttle the *Pronto* by fixing them to the inside of the ship's hull.

The deserted ship was boarded without incident and preparations made for the sinking. Meanwhile, in order to keep a sharp watch all-round and if necessary to retrieve the prize crew at short notice should anything suddenly stumble across us from out of the mist, *UB-39* slowly circled the immobile *Pronto*.

UB-39 was quite close in to the steamer on the second circuit when the coxswain suddenly threw out an arm to the north-east and called to me "There's a steamer coming up." I raised my binoculars and stifled a gasp. My God, what was that? Ahead of the merchantman was a dirty great destroyer! The warship was about two kilometres off. If he saw us now, I had two minutes to get my prize crew off the steamer and submerge. At high speed I put the boat into hiding behind the *Pronto* and gave a whistle with all my strength on the battery-pipes. This was the agreed signal for the prize crew to abandon the Allied ship. Quickly they jumped to it and manned the ship's lifeboat which was fortunately on the same side as the U-boat. Once they had scrambled back aboard I dived without further ado, running off underwater but maintaining a periscope observation of the destroyer and the transport which he was escorting. It seemed he had failed to notice us.

Unfortunately the *Pronto* was still afloat and this had to be rectified. After a while, once the destroyer had passed out of sight, I surfaced and ran back to the steamer. I was presented with the problem of getting the prize crew aboard the derelict again. The two lifeboats had long since drifted off into the mist and the *Pronto* was rolling wildly in the swell. With a brisk manoeuvre I brought *UB-39* within a metre of her side, avoiding a scrape but close enough for Busse and his men to leap across to the overhanging lifeboat davits.

Bearing in mind our earlier surprise, I told Busse to get one of the remaining lifeboats into the water before he started. Once this was done, I resumed circling the steamer. After five minutes a shadow throwing up a huge bow-wave emerged from the fog approximately where I had seen the destroyer and transporter disappear. We stared in horror. The destroyer had apparently taken his charge to a place of safety and was now returning at high speed to deal with me. Destroyer and U-boat were both on the leeside of the *Pronto*. The quickest way for me to take cover was to reverse around the steamer's stern. This manoeuvre brought me about 30 metres clear of the steamer's shadow for a few seconds and the destroyer immediately opened fire with two salvos from all the guns he could bring to bear. The shells dropped so close to the boat that I felt the ironwork trembling at the force of the detonations. Once I slipped behind the steamer, the destroyer ceased fire. Did he do this in case the steamer still had crew-members aboard or because he wanted to preserve her intact for a tow to port? Either way, it was our good fortune. Like a man possessed I blew the recall on the battery-pipe. Three men of the prize crew appeared at the railings in response and called down, "We can't find Leutnant Busse!"

"If you don't find him in fifteen seconds, get off without him. One of you keep reporting what the destroyer is doing," I shouted through the megaphone. U-boat and destroyer could not see each other because the steamer stood between us.

Suddenly the prize crew lookout waved to me madly with

both arms, shouting, "The destroyer is coming straight for us!"

I had to keep my head here. Damn! What was I supposed to do now? Let the prize crew fall into the enemy's hands? My best people? Impossible! I could do nothing but keep whistling the recall on the battery-pipes. The coxswain and I were whistling like madmen. If they didn't come now I would be gambling the boat.

My lookout on the steamer's railings had disappeared. Now I had no idea where I stood. I simply had to know what the destroyer was doing. I ordered immediate dive-readiness and with only the coxswain on the conning tower for company took the boat cautiously beyond the stern of the *Pronto* for a peep at the destroyer. At the same instant the lifeboat appeared under the stern bearing the prize crew, Busse hastily buckling his trouser belt. The other crewmen were pulling mightily at the oars, but the small boat was being forced back by the sea. A warning was being shouted to us, accompanied by furious gesticulations, but it was impossible to make any sense of it. Was the destroyer that close? They seemed to be telling us to leave them to it. At last I caught a sentence. "Destroyer closing in! Go! Go!"

We were in great danger, but I couldn't abandon my brave prize crew. I slewed the submarine round the stern directly towards them, lost control and accidentally rammed the lifeboat. I had left the protection of the steamer and at the moment I came clear the destroyer turned to bring his broadside to bear and fired a salvo. Busse and his men rowed their sinking boat towards us in desperation. Another salvo screamed out from the destroyer. As this second group plunged into the sea on each side of us, we managed to haul the four men aboard, stuffed them down the conning tower, slammed the hatch cover shut and submerged.

At seven metres by the depth gauge there was a terrible crashing, grinding and bursting that left the coxswain ashen-faced. I looked at him aghast. What was that? The boat sank deeper; gradually it became quieter and trim was established safely at forty metres. I thought that we had probably dived too close to the steamer and the conning tower had collided with the ship's keel. Later I confirmed this guess as correct: the bridge was a heap of tangled metal. The main periscope was buckled over at a right angle. The helm and magnetic compass were squashed together. Fortunately the reserve periscope was still intact and we were able to continue the patrol.

Once the boat was quiet I asked Leutnant Busse why he had ignored my recall whistle. He stated that he had not heard it. While aboard the *Pronto* he had had the irresistible urge to visit the master's washroom. Apparently it was such a well-appointed toilet that Busse had quite lost all sense of time and urgency in it!

I was glad to have saved the prize crew. Busse was a splendid young man and I valued especially his proven unflappability in all situations, but this was going a bit too far. One will understand that the dressing-down I gave him was necessarily rather harsh and vulgar. Half an hour later we sat down together over a bottle of port. Busse promised in future to leave his strange addiction strictly ashore.

Chapter 6

HURRICANE AT FORTY METRES

Following every operation in *UB-39* the impression grew stronger that I had at my disposal a really powerful weapon of war. The burden of restrictions respecting the conduct of the U-boat war weighed on us heavily and further limitations continued to be handed down from time to time, but at least we had the satisfaction of knowing that our success had already rendered valuable service to the cause as a whole.

When one considered the possibilities inherent in the U-boat offensive, however, when one saw how this was ultimately the weapon by which the enemy could be bent to our will and the war thus brought to a successful conclusion, when one realized these things and measured what we had been allowed to achieve against what had had to be achieved, only then did the mediocrity of our achievement become apparent. For out there, on the open sea, and especially in the English Channel, when one saw the amount of shipping converging on Britain in an incessant stream, when one saw how busily the enemy was engaged in importing from all quarters of the globe the materials that reinforced his strength for the fight against us, one saw the writing on the wall in a way that was not apparent to people in the homeland, or to the Army, or those in high politics.

How bitter is the knowledge that we actually had it in our

hands to reduce this stream to a trickle, then to have dammed the trickle so that one day the stream would have dried up completely. On that day the enemy would have been compelled to sue for peace. Though undefeated, the Royal Navy would have had to admit defeat. Meanwhile we pursued the shipping war according to the Prize Regulations, laid our mines, sank as much tonnage as we could with our hands tied behind our backs and constantly sought to improve our handling skills.

On her next voyage *UB-39* returned to the operational area in the western English Channel frequented on the previous outing when we had played hide and seek around the *Pronto*. Our tally of successes rose quite handsomely, and then one day there descended upon us from out of the west a storm so severe that I could not remember its like anywhere in the world previously, or since.

The day before it struck, the swell had been so enormous that it had been almost impossible to use the deck gun. Nevertheless we managed to sink one steamer with it despite the difficulties. That night the storm came, and with such force that we were driven to seek refuge in the depths. One huge sea after another reared up above the boat and swept forward to bury the conning tower for ten to twenty seconds at a time. The lookouts could scarcely draw breath and recover from one great mountain of water before the next gigantic sea arrived, and as the boat was swamped by each a deluge poured down through the open bridge hatch into the interior. Accordingly I took the boat to the maximum permissible depth to escape the effects of the storm. I ordered forty metres, but at this depth the sea was still so monstrous that the boat heaved and fell on the slopes and valleys of the moving ranges almost as much as on the surface. At a variety of bizarre angles we were constantly tossed between forty and fifty metres depth by the elements. The exterior control surfaces were utterly ineffective. Each time the boat plunged downwards out of control we were seized by sheer horror. Was this the dive which could not be halted? Would the hull withstand the pressure? We had three thousand metres beneath the keel, no bottom here to catch us safely if we fell.

The hydroplane operators sweated madly in their attempts to

keep the pitching movements of the boat within limits, but the work was so intense that the effort could obviously not be maintained for long. In desperation I angled the submarine broadside to see if that helped, but this seemed even worse, for the pounding was now accompanied by a vile rolling which caused an unimaginably wretched sensation in the confines of such a narrow tube. At the same time the boat continued to rise and fall awkwardly. This was not quite so vicious as when lying into the undertow but it still gave me some anxiety.

The combination of movements was so repulsive that even the hardiest old seafarers in the crew were sea-sick. This did nothing to improve the quality of the fug we were inhaling. I had the air purification system running and released some oxygen into the atmosphere, but we felt our heads would burst all the same.

For the officers and senior ratings there was no question of giving permission for sleep no matter how difficult it might be to keep the eyes open. The behaviour of the boat demanded the fullest attention and watchfulness. After twelve hours we could stand no more. What awaited us on the surface, in the raging storm, the last night had shown. But down here there was fear, fear that the boat would fail, fear that the next sea would be the one to drive the boat to that unknown depth where the hull could withstand the pressure no more and UB-39 would be squashed flat as a bug. Twelve hours we had had this fear and I had had enough of it. Better to weather the storm up there than remain in this hell any longer. Surface!

At twenty metres the boat was seized as if by an invisible hand and tossed to the surface in one motion. Hurriedly I raised the periscope and found myself gazing out upon a scene of indescribably awesome beauty. Before the hurricane great mountains of enormous height and majesty rolled leisurely eastwards, a liquid alpine landscape streaked with spindrift, the air full of flying spray whipped from the wavetops by the shrieking wind.

Whilst enjoying this tremendous spectacle I was judging how the boat reacted to all these natural forces, how she slid down the steepest incline at great speed but then recovered in the trough between two seas, how she valiantly stood before the next great wall of water, high as a church, which bore menacingly down on us with malice in its heart, and how she rose lightly to climb its surface.

I continued to watch these motions for some while, and when I saw how they were repeated endlessly I knew the boat would be able to ride the storm. On account of their height, the trough between two seas was long, which was favourable because the incline was less precipitous and the boat could easily climb it on its approach. This also meant that there would be less sea breaking over the conning tower than at the onset of the storm when the seas were shorter.

I was not proposing to drive into the oncoming sea because of the wind strength and flying spray which would be highly problematical. Instead I chose to run before the sea. Unavoidably, this manoeuvre involved having the hurricane broadside for a few moments and I accepted a grave risk of capsize. Once I had the sea from astern I maintained periscope observation for a few manoeuvres and found the boat wonderfully comfortable at slow ahead, even remaining relatively dry in the raging sea. Later I conned the submarine from the bridge, leaving open the tower hatch cover to aerate the interior.

We had no operable compass. The gyro compass had failed in the violent pounding which the boat had taken and the magnetic compass, which was our reserve, had also succumbed to the storm. This set us the problem of maintaining any sort of course in the raging sea. The helmsman would have to be able to steer by eye which meant using the bridge wheel.

This was easier said than done, as I soon discovered. When these monstrous following seas broke over us, they literally buried the boat several metres under, and the helmsman and I, as the only two men on the bridge, were forced to clutch the nearest convenient projections for dear life to avoid being swept overboard. The solution was both of us to be lashed to the tower upperworks with strapping and rope from which in an emergency we could be slashed free at a moment's notice by a crewman stationed directly below the hatch and holding an open knife. I was right by the open hatch cover and had to kick it shut to prevent the boat being swamped whenever a comber reared up behind us.

It was only possible to proceed on the electric motors. The air for the diesels came through the hatch cover, and when this was shut the engines fed on the remaining air inside the boat until a vacuum was created in which the crew would suffocate to death. There was an air intake mast but in the conditions this was always under water and so the screws had to be battery-driven.

One whole afternoon and night the boat was swept along like this by the mighty sea. The helmsmen were relieved every two hours. This was an extremely tricky process because the man coming off had to be released from his lashings and his relief strapped up in his place. I stayed on the bridge all this time. The boat could be swamped and sunk at any moment if a sharp lookout was not kept and the hatch cover slammed shut in time. I decided there should be three of us up there and had whoever happened to be officer of the watch at the time join me. We had to use sign-language to make ourselves understood as the roaring of the sea and the howling wind made spoken communication impossible.

Late that afternoon we passed close alongside a very fat steamer. We waved up as we surged by. It must have been obvious to him that no attack was possible in the conditions, but we probably gave the freighter's master a nasty shock when he saw us so near. Our 30-metre-long boat would have been hidden amongst the waves until the last moment.

Towards morning the hurricane slackened off and the seas gradually became lower, although there was a huge swell. As this would inevitably persist for a few days, probably depriving us of any opportunity for an attack, I decided to head for home.

Off Cape Barfleur, east of Cherbourg, a heavily laden steamer hove into view. This vessel looked so enticing that I decided to make an attack despite the high swell. I worked round into a favourable position of wind and sea and opened fire. The steamer bore 45° to starboard on a course that would have eventually brought him across our bow, but stood off immediately as our first shells plumed up in the water and almost at once he returned fire from a weapon on his poop deck. His aim was abysmal, but ours was little better because the swell was too high for accurate shooting. After a short while the steamer made another course change to bring him head on to the seas and I was obliged to come round as well in order to keep my deck gun trained on him. Our chances were now much less favourable because the bows were rising and plunging into the swell, but all I needed was one lucky hit in his engine room to bring him to a standstill and this spurred me on.

I had sunk my teeth into this merchantman and was holding on with a grim stubbornness. He was astute, forcing me to make more and more adjustments to my course to keep him within the arc of fire of the deck gun, and I knew that I was being outmanoeuvred. I had just altered another couple of degrees and was observing the steamer through my binoculars when my attention was attracted by some desperate cries from the area of the forecasing. I glanced at the gun and saw it was unmanned. At the same time there was a shout, "Men overboard!" and at once I saw three members of the five-man gun crew swimming alongside, the other two having managed to reboard. A curling crest had come foaming along the forecasing and swept them all over the side. The steamer was forgotten. We were able very quickly to haul two of the three on board, but the third, the gun captain, had drifted some distance away from the boat.

At once I had to sort out the best way of getting at him. Submarines are notoriously unwieldy craft, especially in a rough sea. I would have preferred to have stood off and come round to him in a large curve but I was sure I would lose sight of him in the high swell. This left me with no choice but to saw backwards and forwards through the seas using the rudder to edge the boat closer to the man in the water. Every time I thought we had him, a sea would intervene and separate us again. Lines and lifebelts were thrown but he was kitted out in full leather garb and was too exhausted treading water to reach them. I kept up the manoeuvring but always he was drifting further away from us and I began to see the belief written in his face that he was lost. From time to time he would vanish from sight as a sea buried him, then he would appear, gasping, swallowing air and water in a desperate fight for breath.

Bathed in sweat I stood on the tower watching this dire struggle, ever mindful of the need to issue helm and engine commands calmly. I used every free moment to bellow down encouragement such as "Keep your head up, son! Pay attention, watch what you're doing! We're soon going to have you in!" and a string of similar inane instructions, the idea being to keep him conscious, to keep hope alive. He wore no lifejacket: if he lost consciousness he would drown.

Then a great sea approached. I had to give first priority to the boat. The man was hurled against the side, he saw the eager hands reach out to grasp him, thought himself saved, fainted . . . and was swept away.

At the last moment, Leutnant Busse, who had sprinted the length of the fore-deck, threw himself down full length at the bow, made a despairing lunge and got a hand on the man's clothing. And thus he was saved.

The steamer was by now well out of range; there was no question of a chase. In any case I had had enough of this particular patrol, I just wanted to get home. This presented some problems. I had no compass and I was forced to follow the French coast eastwards, making frequent detours whenever an enemy patrol hove into sight. By the evening of the twelfth day out we dead-reckoned our position as twenty miles south-west of Boulogne.

Now came the tricky part, to get through the unlit Straits of Dover by night, surfaced and without a compass. Fortunately the sky was clear and we could see the pole star. The helmsman, who throughout had been steering from the bridge, had to keep the star at a particular angle corresponding to a heading of 60° magnetic. In the powerful current running in the Strait and with frequent changes of course to avoid detection by enemy naval vessels and anti-submarine-net picket boats, this was a very rough and ready sort of navigation. We had had some good luck on this voyage and it did not desert us for our passage of the Strait. Once we were through, Mother Sun rose and showed us the way to the coast of Flanders. Next evening we arrived safe and well at Bruges.

Chapter 7

"I'VE JUST GOT THIS FEELING I OUGHT TO BE CAREFUL"

At last it had arrived! Unrestricted U-boat warfare began. It seemed as if we had been unchained. We had lost a burden we had carried since the day war broke out. We were officers of a Navy of which the principal fighting strength, the High Seas Fleet, had lain idle for months on end or – and it was not possible to shrug off the impression – had not been deployed in the manner it ought to have been. In the U-boat Arm the compensation lay in the special assignments which were increasingly falling to our lot. The longer these assignments continued, and the more difficult they were, the more there began to develop a bond between crew and boat in the sense that the human organism, eyes, ears, muscles, nerves and intelligence were components of the U-boat. With the enormous possibilities which the new weapon offered we came to know our own possibilities, capabilities and limitations. On these long missions, each crewman underwent a transformation and gradually developed into a true U-boat man.

The U-boat man, what is that? When attempting to explain this term, I think of my shallow sleep. I got used to this kind of rest aboard *U-20*, the first U-boat on which I served as watch officer. Although my bunk was in the forward torpedo room just aft of the tubes, I would always know when something was amiss. No matter how exhausted I might be when falling asleep, I would awaken immediately if there was a problem in the control room, even if the only indication was someone's slightly raised voice. I knew in my sleep if the boat was trimmed slightly more by the head or stern than she should have been. Essentially I did not have a true sleep because I did not allow my U-boat consciousness to disengage as I slept. I experienced the boat because there was no real separation between our identities. I was not her commander, but I felt as responsible for the boat as for myself. Nothing must happen to the boat! The feeling was that only if one cared for her personally, at all times, would she be safe. If all was well with the boat, one dreamt, what might become of one personally did not enter into it.

Responsibility is a strange thing. There is not much to be said about it: one either has it or not. Yet there are moments when one may say of it, it was precisely then that I experienced the feeling of responsibility. During a patrol in which I was one of the boat's watch officers and Half-Flotilla Chief Gayer was also aboard, *U-20* had a certain stern-heaviness which was not normal. I awoke, sat up in my bunk and thought, 'The commander is awake, and the Half-Flotilla Chief is also there'. But all the same, it didn't feel right to me. I looked down the long boat as if through a long cylinder and saw the two of them standing together in concern. I heard them say, "We ought to fetch the watch officer." I ran down to the control room, quickly identified the fault and corrected it. Straightforward, but such moments as these leave their mark. From then on I was on hand like a gundog when anything was awry in the boat. I felt it in my bones and was always there at once. This sense of always being aware was the best possible preparation for my time as commander.

So now, in February 1917, Germany had declared unrestricted U-boat warfare. We would have six months, so they said, to pull it off. In these six months we would have to give everything we had to force the Allies to the negotiating table. Germany's hopes had been placed into the hands of the U-boat Arm. We had been entrusted with an endeavour imbued with the highest level of responsibility, to commit ourselves to the uttermost for Germany. We could not ask more from Destiny than that.

That unrestricted submarine warfare had at last been introduced was due in no small degree to the committedness, unceasing effort and indomitable resolution of the Commanding Officer of the Flanders U-Flotilla, Korvettenkapitän Bartenbach, who even pre-war had contributed so much to the development of the U-boat Arm.

After the occupation of Flanders, Bartenbach had created first-class U-boat bases from what had been purely makeshift installations at Bruges and Ostend. The Flanders U-boat Flotilla had initially been set up merely to defend the coast of Flanders, but he had developed from these modest beginnings the strategic attack Flotilla which would ultimately bear the brunt of Germany's aspirations. Yet over and above even this was the significance of his recent achievement at the political level.

Naturally we U-boat people had all come to the Flanders U-Flotilla buoyant with enthusiasm. We made our voyages; we made voyages that were increasingly more difficult, and soon there was not one amongst us who had not escaped death and destruction by the skin of his teeth on more than one occasion.

These unpleasant realities soon made hard men of us, men accustomed to braving the elements and the enemy with dogged determination, for whom a mere Hurrah! on returning to port was no recompense for what we had been required to endure. Bartenbach recognized that more was needed to maintain our inner strengths for the greatest performance. It was Bartenbach who installed in us the highest clarity of purpose, a wild hatred, an iron will and a readiness for self-sacrifice bound up with love for the soil of the homeland. This holy ardour, this spirit of the Flanders U-Flotilla, was to be the foundation stone for our success and the terrorization of our enemies.

It is the paradox of the *Führer der U-boote* that he must always lead in battle from the rear. In harbour, however, he was not only with us but lived among us. There he was the highly esteemed confidante of all while still managing to remain aloof from us as FdU. It was from this closeness to the men at the Front, a contact-keeping with the practical side of the U-boat war combined with a clear overall appreciation of affairs, that he derived his deep-seated conviction to argue strenuously the case for unrestricted U-boat warfare.

He was fully committed to this objective and often encountered stern opposition but fought on resolutely. He had an heroic ally in Admiral von Schröder, Chief of the Naval Corps, who lent him support on a number of occasions. It was therefore natural for our part that, when the goal was finally achieved, we should see this primarily as Bartenbach's victory and therefore rejoice doubly.

I embarked upon the new era of unrestricted U-boat warfare in a new boat. In November 1916 I was entrusted with the command of *UC-70* after having relinquished, with a heavy heart, my beloved *UB-39* to an especially able and dear comrade, Oberleutnant zur See Küstener. As had been the case with the earlier boat, I commissioned *UC-70* at the Blohm & Voss Yard and after successful trials brought her round the coast to Flanders in the spring of 1917.

UC-70 was an improved version of the small U-minelayer, a further improvement on the Type which the Flanders U-Flotilla had used to such a good effect and against which the British had been forced to such lengths to combat. By reason of their limited range these boats had had to operate no further than the south-east coast of England, where nevertheless they had regularly obtained valuable successes.

It was a great pity that the Type was unsuitable to carry out minelaying operations at all points along the British coastline. The idea that a policy of unrestricted submarine warfare might be pursued at some stage in the future had filtered through relatively early into certain influential circles and led to the design and construction of a new Type of minelaying U-boat which, although it did not have a much improved minelaying capacity, did at least boast an engine plant which brought the whole British coastline within its range.

My *UC-70* was one of these new boats. The Type displaced 450 tons instead of 160 tons, carried eighteen mines instead of twelve, was fitted with one underwater and two surface torpedo tubes and an 8.8-cm deck gun. The powerful diesels provided a top speed of twelve knots. The boat was capable of remaining below much longer than the C-boat and was considerably more habitable.

One of the first voyages I made in *UC-70* was to Biscay in March 1917. My mission was first to lay a mine barrage off the Île de Groix, Le Four and Point de Chassiron and then attack shipping. The priority target was troop transports from the United States. It was being assumed that these vessels would prefer French Biscay ports as this would provide them with the quickest means of getting their men to the Front.

I laid my mines within the first few days of my arrival in the operational area and then took up the search for American troop transports in earnest. I considered that Bordeaux was the most likely disembarkation port on the French west coast and hung around there just out of sight of the coast for several days. When nothing appeared I moved in closer.

The only vessel I saw was a large French pilot cutter flying her identification flag from a mast-top. She came out from a small town right at the mouth of the Gironde Estuary. Its red roofs shone in the midday sun. As there was nothing better in sight I thought I might as well knock off this two-masted schooner. I decided to have a little fun first by approaching him to within thirty metres under water and then frightening the wits out the crew by surfacing right alongside. Unfortunately it was not the crew of the pilot cutter who got the shock.

The order to surface was on my lips when the helmsman of the pilot cutter came to the vessel's side nearest me, dropped his trousers and more or less stuck his bottom in my face. At least, this was how it appeared to me as I peered through the periscope with a 6 x magnification at a distance of 30 metres. I retracted the periscope stick in embarrassment and, out of respect for the call of nature, postponed my attack until the man had finished his business.

Once a decent time had elapsed, I surfaced. The pilot had just lit a short pipe and started in horror at the sudden appearance of this monster snorting up from the deep, so I had my amusement after all. We made short work of the cutter. It seemed a very large schooner to be manned by only two men. They rowed to the coast in their lifeboat with a very gloomy demeanour.

The pilot cutter had been loafing around for the sake of appearances. There was no shipping around Bordeaux and in vain I waited for US troop transports to appear. At nightfall I headed northwards and by daybreak I was lurking to the south of the island of Oléron where the prospects of finding a troop-ship were about as bleak as Bordeaux.

Around 0900 I came across a bunch of large two-masted schooners of the French deep-sea fleet. Once in their midst, I used their dories to ferry my prize crews from one schooner to the next, sinking them as they went. Within ninety minutes we had finished. Twelve large schooners, each with holds brimming with fish, lay wrecked on the sea bed. The loss of the fish, and more so the fishing boats, would make an impression on French food supplies. While engaged in disposing of the last schooner, a French naval craft opened fire on us on its way out from the coast, although this did not prevent me from completing the job in hand. I was not keen to submerge and, as I would be greatly disadvantaged by the high swell that was running if I decided to battle it out with the gun, I made a run for it to the open sea and the patrol vessel soon appeared to lose interest.

We had been making offshore for about half an hour when two more schooners of the same type hove into view on the star-board bow, heading straight into our arms. The next schooner we sank would be the thirteenth of the day. So – watch out! The first twelve had been a piece of cake. This time I had the gun manned the ammunition brought up and sent all the crew, with the exception of the men on the gun and on lookout, to diving stations. When dealing with this schooner I wanted the boat to be in the highest state of battle- and dive-readiness. Really, I had to laugh at myself over the measures I was taking, and even my watch officer ribbed me for being so gutless about the number thirteen.

"I've just got this feeling I ought to be careful," I told him, "and now we'll find out. If I've been barking up the wrong tree, you'll have a bottle of port for the trouble. But all the same, maximum alert."

71

Meanwhile the wind had freshened and the two oncoming schooners were moving along very smartly. I was surprised that they were keeping so steadfastly to their course, for they must have seen us. They would pass at about 150 metres abeam.

When there was only 500 metres between us, I shouted down to the watch officer, who was supervising the gun crew, "Fire a shot over the bow of the leading schooner to get him to heave-to." The gun barked once, and a column of water plumed up fifty metres ahead of his track. But those stolid French fishermen appeared not to have noticed, for their vessel continued dourly on its course – helmsmen astern, lookout on the fore-peak, just as on the other fishing boats. We were within 150 metres. As I had another look at him through my binoculars four or five men sprang out from below decks, threw off a large canvas cover amidships, cleared a deck gun, aimed at us and opened fire.

I had roared down "Rapid fire!" Our gun replied and knocked down his forward rig and tackle with the first round. Good! The next couple of shells would sink the swine; it was not necessary to dive or turn away. Now we poured out shot after shot at the sailing vessel. At this range we were aiming over open sights; we could have hit her with a hail of potatoes, she was so close. In the excitement, and because the high swell hid the schooner's hull from sight for seconds at a time, our fire became so ragged that everything was falling wide, short or over. Through the binoculars I could see the business end of the enemy's gun barrel growing ever larger. His fire was extremely quick and accurate, and the range was so short that we ducked immediately whenever we saw a flash of fire at the muzzle trained on us.

Every shot made a loud crack. Almost at once he would get a hit somewhere on our hull. Only the thought that our next shot, or maybe the one after, would hit him in a vital spot spurred me on. We had to hit him!

Suddenly there was a hissing somewhere in the hull; it grew louder, became a gurgle. I had the impression we were lower in the water. Another crack, the shock on my ear-drums, people screaming nearby. Streaming with blood at my side was the telegraphist. He had been relaying a shell and dropped it, his right hand almost torn off by a splinter. He staggered against me. I couldn't hold him up and he collapsed. I got him to the bridge hatch and heard voices shouting up urgently from the deck gun, "We're nearly all of us wounded down here, Herr Oberleutnant!", and at the same time from the control room. "The boat's sinking. We must have sprung a leak!"

"Fast dive!" I shouted down to the gun crew, and at once blood-streaked figures leaning against each other for support pushed past me and toppled down the open hatch in a daze. The tower was slippery with blood, almost every man slipped and fell on descending. I followed close behind the last man, jumped through the hatch as the boat submerged, lost my footing, managed to grab the hatch cover, pulled it shut above me, then cried out "Flood! Hard to port! Go to thirty metres!"

I heard a strange hissing and gurgling in the boat; the control room was in utter confusion. I kept shouting "Flood! As quickly as you can, flood!" Everything depended on getting below and avoiding any more hits. Then the noises in the boat got so loud I could no longer make myself heard.

At last the Chief Engineer understood what I needed to know: report if we had received a hit where the water was gurgling into the boat and if the leak could be held. Engineer Dietrich rushed off, returned after a few moments and roared, "Pressure hull undamaged!"

Thank God! Everything was in total disarray but at least we could trim the boat at 30 metres. We had to: there was nearly a thousand metres beneath the keel. A terrible thing to be crushed to death by the water pressure in a dive that could not be stopped.

Things were slowly beginning to return to normal. First I obtained confirmation that the hydroplanes were operating normally. Fortunately the forward operator had been only lightly wounded at the gun; the stern hydroplane was manned by a stoker who had not been above deck. The Chief Engineer was supervising them. This was normally the job of the watch officer but he was too badly wounded to continue, sitting on his bunk, his face covered in blood, holding his head in his hands, softly groaning "My God, my God". But there were two cases far worse than him, so we had to leave him to it.

First of all we bandaged telegraphist Lindemann who had lost all his right hand between the thumb and little finger. We had stopped the bleeding and the man was whimpering, huddled up in a corner. I knew that he was thinking about his trade; he was a precision engineer. But there would be much worse to come soon, for the real pain of the wound would set in only later. I tried to comfort him as best I could and then we made a bed for him where he was.

In a bunk further forward was a rating, a fresh, blond youth, unconscious with loss of blood. He had received a quite small splinter of shrapnel in an artery in the neck. Blood was pouring out of the wound and couldn't be stopped. The dressing was tight, but was soon soaked through although it had been applied in several layers. What else could one do? Perhaps we weren't doing it properly. We had all been trained in first aid theory, but had no practice.

Then I remembered Leading Seaman Skotzky. His first voyage aboard *UC-70*, Skotzky had come on the muster from the Naval Corps and had taken part in all the recent heavy Flanders battles. He would be sure to know something about the treatment of wounds!

Skotzky was at the helm, a strong, rather stocky young man with clear blue eyes. He came quietly and confidently, looked at the casualty for a moment and then said, "We have to wrap it really well, Herr Oberleutnant, lay the bandages on until his head looks like a pumpkin. Somehow that stops the bleeding." We could all sense his authority. Skotzky could do something that we couldn't, which was to apply a dressing correctly. In addition, he was a marvellous fellow, sensible and strong as a bear. He had phenomenal eyesight and was the best lookout aboard. Skotzky wound and wound, and we wound too, packing everything we had around it, and finally no more blood was seeping through. Was it the dressing or had the man no more blood to lose? I didn't know, but I could at least pass on to the next patient in a calmer frame of mind.

Together with Skotzky, next I examined the watch officer.

74

Initially we could find nothing under his hair, matted with blood, but then we discovered a few very tiny, nasty pieces of shrapnel in his scalp. We managed to extract five of these slivers, which caused the casualty terrible pain, but we had to leave another four where they were as our instruments were too basic for the task. Actually the wounds didn't look too bad, but he must have been in great agony, for he was babbling incoherently. I considered it justifiable to open the morphine dispensary, which was under my personal control, and injections were administered to those who needed them. After that the excitement began to subside and gradually it grew calmer.

How we were to nurse these casualties would be a problem for later. Apart from the worst cases there were two walking wounded who would be absent from duty for several more days. This was a major depletion of our small complement. But first I had to determine the condition of the boat. The Chief Engineer made his report. It was his opinion that the dive tanks had been punctured at many points, permitting the escape of compressed air. While the gun battle had been raging above, it had been obvious in the control room that the boat was gradually settling deeper for this reason. The piping of six compressed air bottles had been shot up, as could be confirmed from the depth gauge. We had lost two-thirds of our compressed air reserve, which was what we absolutely relied upon for our safety. This was very bad. Now I knew that as we dived the gurgling noise which I had taken for the sound of inrushing water had been the compressed air escaping.

During the 45 minutes we had been submerged I had steered a course directly into the surface wind direction to ensure that, if the damage to the pressure hull forced us to the surface, the armed ketch would have her work cut out to get to grips with us again. I had put a few miles' sea room between the two vessels and deemed it safe to come up to periscope depth. It was essential to surface as soon as possible to ventilate the boat, which smelt like a field-hospital, and to establish visually the extent of the external damage. I made a full circle of the horizon with the periscope. We were alone. Perhaps the enemy sailing vessel had also had enough for one day.

I ordered the dive-tanks amidships to be blown using the available compressed air in order at least to get the upper casing above sea level. The engineer kept on blowing but the casing remained below the surface. The uppermost metre of the conning tower projected above the surface and no more than this could be achieved; the casing remained two metres down. If we were unable to get any more buoyancy than this we were finished! Despite the swell I opened up the hatch and climbed out. The sea was reasonably calm, just the occasional crest which broke over the hatch, but this had to be tolerated. So as not to waste any more of our precious compressed air, I gave orders to try blowing the dive tanks using the engines. Once this was started, I observed how the stream of air which was supposed to force out the water ballast from the dive tanks gurgled up to the surface beforehand in huge bubbles. Obviously the piping had been shot to pieces!

During consultation with the Chief Engineer, it was recalled that we had a back-up device which the U-boat Inspectorate had insisted on installing as a precautionary measure, but which we had never needed to use previously – the so-called Emergency Shut-Off Valves. These were located on the dive-tanks and made it possible for them to be blown using compressed air even if the main piping had been punctured. By use of these valves, within a relatively short space of time the water from the dive-tanks was expelled and the boat surfaced fully.

UC-70 was alone on the sea, the sun laughed down from a clear blue sky, our wounded were as well as could be expected in the circumstances, and with a will our engineers set about repairing the damaged piping. We had sustained serious shell damage in six places but miraculously the pressure hull had survived intact. The thread by which we had clung to life had been a very fine one.

Two days we drifted on the bosom of the deep blue Atlantic while work proceeded at a feverish pace to get us diveworthy. Never once did we observe the slightest trace of another vessel and this was just as well, for it would have taken four times longer than normal to submerge, and once below our troubles would only begin. But at last the repairs were finished. The worst effects of the six hits had been eliminated and after a fashion the piping had been restored. *UC-70* was diveable. Considering the limited materials we had aboard, Dietrich and his people had almost done the impossible in these few days, an achievement I would not easily forget.

We set off for port. I was on tenterhooks. Our tally of wounded meant that we were short of five hands from a ship's company of twenty-five, and we had the additional labour of working the heavy emergency shut-off valves. At least on the first day of the homeward voyage we had a reason for rejoicing. The rating with the wound to the temple, who until then had been unconscious and for whom we entertained the gravest fears, suddenly opened his eyes, looked around him and then said softly, but distinctly, "Children, I'm hungry." He was spoonfed, and from day to day began to recover his strength.

The boat snaked through the English Channel with the greatest possible caution; we could not afford any breakdown in the emergency repairs in those waters. We breathed a little more freely once the boat stood eastward of the Dover Strait, having survived a number of unpleasant moments, but only when we dropped our cables over the bollards at Bruges did we feel that we had really survived the patrol.

No boat had ever previously made it home in such a state. On behalf of the crew I accepted many congratulations for having managed to sail the wreck to port and kept alive all our seriously wounded. Privately I knew of course that we had been dangling from a silken thread over the edge of a precipice.

Our wounded were hospitalized at once. The watch officer with skull shrapnel underwent a number of serious operations. He was never again fit for duty, nor was the rating with the serious head wound. Telegraphist Lindemann's injury turned gangrenous and he too required much surgery, although at least he also survived the war. Later I visited him in hospital at Braunschweig and was overjoyed to see that he had come to terms with his wounds and had regained his former cheerfulness.

Chapter 8

EGG-LAYING WITH *UC-70*

After having expended a great deal of effort laying a small mine-field off Le Havre in the position prescribed in our operational orders, *UC-70* was now on the lurk for a convoy to attack, preferably under the cover of darkness. I took up position north of Ushant on the north-west corner of France, which our agents had reported to be the French end of the convoy route from Portland. A heavy swell set in during the early hours and continued to strengthen so that the boat, motoring at low speed, rolled and pounded alarmingly. This was the harbinger of a strong westerly gale which reached us about midday. Our course was diagonal to the sea direction and the boat was so lively in the conditions that it became distinctly unpleasant. I was rarely seasick nowadays, since I had grown accustomed to the sea, but nevertheless I still felt as sick as a dog, and experi-enced those depths of morale and thought such as can only arise in low physical states.

I braced myself against the bridge coaming to avoid being thrown around. I cursed the evil spray, which would suddenly come flying into my face or neck, but I knew how much worse it would be for me if I descended into the fuel oil stink inside the boat. I prayed for some feverish activity to arouse me from this terrible listlessness, but the horizons were empty of all but the roaring, foaming wave-crests. Gazing out on this tumult of nature, I pictured in my mind's eye the millpond conditions in which we had laid our mines off Le Havre. Heaven knows, a sea like a mirror was ordinarily the last thing we wished for for U-boat handiwork, and especially not when sowing mines on an enemy coast. That was something we had found out only too well off Le Havre. It was nothing short of a miracle that everything had eventually gone as planned.

It was our task to lay twelve mines in the navigable channel shorewards of the lightship moored just clear of the harbour entrance. In order to set the mines at the most effective depth, the state of the tide had to be allowed for and the boat had to be ready to drop the mines at 2330 hrs on that particular evening.

In the first place, it had been no easy matter to reach the Fécamp lighthouse, from where we had a fix for Le Havre, by the scheduled time. The air was absolutely calm and this, together with the enormous visibility, was very unfavourable for an approach unseen. We were frequently forced to submerge which greatly reduced our speed of advance towards the objective.

We made Fécamp eventually with not a moment to spare. At dusk we steered for Le Havre. If possible I wanted to lay the mines while surfaced. Soon we were standing close in to the coast, occasionally passing in the vicinity of the odd fishing boat with navigation lanterns weakly lit, when suddenly to starboard I spotted a low shadow on the water. It was a French MTB. We turned away hard, stopped both diesels as they were making too much noise and switched to electric drive. Two more MTBs became visible. We were caught between them and the coast, I had no choice but to submerge, however undesirable that was. Once under water at night in conditions like these, it would be no easy matter to resurface in a busy harbour area like Le Havre.

I spent half an hour on the bottom, then came up to periscope depth. The night was black as pitch; now and again I glimpsed the weak lights from the Fécamp tower and the Le Havre lightship. Submerged, a U-boat has only one eye, and this provided us with only the murkiest impression of what was above us. The question was, should I risk it? If I did, I had to be ready for confrontation with a large number of possible emergencies, not least of which was to come up in the vicinity of an enemy patrol boat or directly in the path of a steamer or warship. In either case we would be as good as done for if I failed to size up the situation in a flash and neglected to take the correct evasive measures. In the event I decided to risk surfacing. I had to attempt to lay the mines from the surface, for, submerged, the boat would use a great deal of electric current. It went without saying that in the prevailing weather conditions at any time we might have desperate need of the batteries, for in this heavily patrolled bay we were likely to be forced to submerge regularly enough anyway.

Therefore, surface! Before giving the order, I had the tower lighting switched off to allow the eyes of coxswain and commander to become accustomed to the darkness; emerging on the bridge we had to see everything around us in a split second. After a short while I gave the order to surface. Compressed air hissed through the piping and roared into the dive tanks. I stood ready on the ladder, hands grasping the bridge hatch, the coxswain close behind me. As soon as the control room reported the tower clear, I released the hatch clips and the lid more or less flew open under the excess air pressure from within the boat. I jumped out and with my first look round saw that there was nothing in the immediate vicinity. Next we had a search with the binoculars.

"There's something," coxswain Kiefer called out, "four points to starboard!"

I swept the glasses round to the bearing indicated; there was a low shadow on the water gradually receding. To port a few dimmed lights flickered in the distance, probably fishing vessels. There was too much naval activity to enable us to proceed fully surfaced, therefore we continued flooded down with only the conning tower above water.

After a while I spotted two dark shadows directly ahead on the placid sea. These were two small torpedo-boats and, as we could not pass by them, I gave the order to submerge. I swore softly . . .

Obviously it was not going to be possible to make further progress on the surface, and I had to be prepared to make the run to the Le Havre lightship and sow the mines while submerged, a task requiring the greatest precision, because there was only sixteen metres' depth at the spot where we were supposed to lay them. The laying was to be done over the bow, and as each mine was almost two metres in diameter, I had to ensure a minimum of three metres of water below the keel to ensure the boat passed clear overhead of each one we dropped. During submerged travel this would mean thirteen metres tideway depth to allow the uppermost point of the boat a clearance of at least five metres below the surface. We would be laying the mines in the busiest navigation channel where the danger of being rammed by a heavily laden steamer was quite acute. The seabed near the lightship was littered with large wrecks and we could easily collide or become entangled with one of these. Therefore we were menaced from above and below the waves and I had so little enthusiasm for conducting the proceedings under water that I made one final try for the surface. Unfortunately I placed the boat directly in the path of an oncoming unlit steamer and only by the sharpest emergency dive was the fatal collision avoided. There was nothing for it but to stay below.

I increased speed, for haste was called for if we were to be in the right position shorewards of the lightship by 2330 hrs precisely. The boat trembled in protest at the high revolutions of the electric motors. Our calculations showed that we might be there a little late; we had to make our maximum submerged speed. The boat was shuddering so much that I wondered whether it would hold together. With stopwatch in hand we counted down the minutes. We would have to keep this up for half an hour before we were there, before the accursed minelaying could begin. The minutes ticked away like small eternities. At last we arrived. With a quick glance through the periscope I confirmed the bearing of the lightship and ordered the course change which would bring us along the track to be mined. The great black spheres were cleared for laying, and at slow speed the boat rose to the dangerous thirteen metres mark.

The submarine jolted as the first mine tumbled out of the shaft. Sixty metres later the second followed, then the third. A large steamer was approaching quickly, her screws pounding massively. Would they grind into our conning tower? I had no time to worry about it. With a thump the fifth mine fell. I had to be deaf to everything happening above and below us, I had to refuse to listen to it. I counted the minutes and I counted the mines we were ejecting, and concentrated everything on the job in hand. I had to get rid of twelve mines, and the nearer came the magic number, the lighter became the facial expressions of those who knew how dangerous this operation was.

Almost on the stroke of midnight the task was completed, and I took the boat seawards at once. Several times the keel touched bottom at seventeen or eighteen metres before the seabed shelved deeply, allowing us to slip quickly away from the lightship, relieved to have this accursed job behind us. We had enough current for two hours' electric drive before being forced to surface to recharge the batteries.

When the two hours were up, we surfaced. For heaven's sake, there were two more MTBs in the immediate vicinity and we still had this millpond of a sea. So, back down again. Twenty minutes later we came up once more. Nothing had changed. I yelled a strongly-worded curse, but to no avail; swearing could not influence the weather gods. I laid the boat on the bottom. The batteries were almost empty. I sat it out in the cellar waiting for a deterioration in the weather so that the MTBs would put back for shelter and let us recharge in peace.

We spent the remainder of the night and almost the whole of the next day on the bottom until the unbreathable fug in the boat forced us to break surface for air. We were greeted by the most satisfactory sight of a rough, white-crested sea devoid of other vessels, the French coast a blur in the distance.

That night *UC-70* headed west for the operational area, a raging wilderness which we reached next day and in which the boat was skewered up, down and around mercilessly. We had despaired at the duckpond off Le Havre, but this was every bit as bad, and was accompanied with the added likelihood of torpedo damage.

At dusk I steered at low speed on a course for Ushant, from where the convoys for England were reported to sail. The night was as black as pitch. How were we supposed to find a ship in this darkness, on the endless sea, across which we could peer no more than half a mile? And with this mad pitching up and down, which made the eyes so weary. I had jammed myself into a spot between the periscope housing and the bridge coaming so as to have my arms free to hold the binoculars, but with the mad gyrations of the boat it was still a labour of Hercules to keep the glasses levelled at the horizon. Actually it was a pointless task in the conditions but it had to be attempted no matter how hopeless it might seem.

We were standing close enough in to the French coast to see the Ushant light and then three points on the starboard quarter a small light blinked. It was to windward of us, and when I steered to investigate the boat rose and fell into seas of substantial height which rolled lazily towards us, regularly swamping the bridge. This forced me to heave-to to reconnoitre, and now suddenly instead of the single occulting light I could see a whole string of lights in the distance, all approximately the same distance apart. These could only be the stern lights of a convoy. What a stroke of luck! Galvanized into action, I gave no further thought to the violent pitching up and down and the seas which swamped us. Now there was a job to do! First of all I had to get *UC-70* windward of the convoy. This meant driving into a head sea. We were soon soaked, but after two hours of effort the flock, unsuspecting, was at my mercy. I manoeuvred the boat between escorts and steamers and torpedoed two of the latter in quick succession before diving to escape a destroyer which was hot on our trail.

When I surfaced ten minutes later the lights had been extinguished, the night was dark and of the convoy there was no longer a sign. I steered a course seawards which gave as comfortable a ride as possible while enabling a sharp lookout to be maintained. Shortly after midnight the gale died away and by morning there was only a heavy swell to remind us of it.

A day later south of Brest we were swallowed up by a sea mist so thick that I had no option but to cut the engines and wallow, waiting for it to lift. For two days we drifted, listening into the opaque curtain for the ship that might run us down.

On the third day it seemed to clear a little, and I ordered slow ahead. On the bridge we wedged ourselves into a comfortable nook and peered through our binoculars into the drifting swathes of fog. After a while the boatswain broke the silence. "Four points to port shadow of a large steamer; ahead of him probable destroyer," he said nonchalantly.

By the time the shadows had taken on a firm shape I saw that they were closing fast and I gave the order to dive away quickly. As soon as we were under I raised the periscope and swept the horizon for several minutes but failed to obtain a sighting of the quarry. Possibly the fog was thicker at the surface than a few metres higher from where we had made the observation. With no prospect of attacking, I abandoned the idea with a clear conscience and took the boat down to twenty metres. We could well be in the path of a convoy and a risk of collision existed. Once the boat was trimmed I set course at slow ahead for the French coast about thirty sea miles distant and then settled comfortably into my bunk. It was still early, and my steward prepared my table for breakfast before fetching a frying pan in which two large fried eggs were sizzling and gurgling.

"Man, Tiede," I croaked for joy, "what are these golden orbs which brighten our miserable abode this morning?" He suppressed a smile and reported, "Herr Oberleutnant, the cook says we have to use up the stock of eggs as soon as possible as some have gone off." Obviously the least time wasted the better then, I thought, and picked up my cutlery. The first egg was balanced on my fork, ready to be shovelled home in the accepted seafarer's fashion when such a jolt rocked the boat that I fell off my bed. We had hit an obstruction. As we were miles from land and had at least 1000 metres below the keel, I assumed we had collided with heavy wreckage, but, even so, twenty metres seemed to be a strange depth for even a sunken wooden vessel to be keeping. Casting a last regretful look at my undevoured fried eggs and reflecting on the caprices of fate I entered the control room. *UC-70* was now thumping continually into the obstruction and I suspected that we must have run aground in uncharted shallows and would have to surface to refloat.

"Go quickly to fifteen metres," I ordered. The shuddering persisted.

"Go to ten metres." At this depth the thudding was still relentless.

"Full astern both, blow tanks amidships!" I cried as I climbed the ladder into the tower.

Once the bridge was clear, I threw open the hatch cover and looked out. In horror I saw that we were grounding and dragging in a heavy surf about thirty metres from a sandy beach. White-capped seas were sweeping inshore over the conning tower. There were rocky outcrops at each end of the beach and if the boat slewed she would be wrecked. I roared out the order for full astern, so close to disaster that I felt my scalp prickle. At last the screws began to bite and we inched sternwards out to deeper water.

From a distance of 200 metres I took a good look at our landfall. It was a horseshoe bay with a spit of sand flanked by a rocky coastline and we had been driven ashore to touch ground in the only spot which would not have ripped open the hull. There was a fishing village built terrace-like into the rock, while on the beach two fishermen, shag-pipes in hand, had paused to stare, open-mouthed, at the iron sea-monster which had suddenly appeared from beneath the waves. Further along a lighthouse keeper was eyeing us carefully, trying to decide whether we were friend or foe. The entire village began to assemble quickly on the beach, staring at us dumbly since they still had no idea with whom they had the honour, while for my part I was most anxious to reach deeper water and get clear of the inshore skerries.

While drawing back offshore I gave orders below to clear for battle and, as soon as we had freedom to manoeuvre, I gave the alarm and steered for the coast again. The gun crew came up from the interior and were making their way to the cannon when plumes of water from a salvo of five shells reared up around us within the 100-200 metre mark but well wide, the report from the guns being audible a second or so later. Our attention was drawn at once to the lighthouse, below which a battery of five field guns was installed, their muzzles flashing red and orange to send the second salvo in our direction; these were also wide but not much. We were outgunned and I had to submerge.

Thus we had lost two of our proverbial nine lives. If the French lookouts of the Ile de Seine had known what a German U-boat looked like we would have been shot to pieces. The only question which remained was to establish why we had stranded on the coast when our navigation put us twenty miles offshore. With the coxswain I checked the trigonometry but found no error. We had been unable to take a sun or star sight for three days on account of the fog and, having failed to allow adequately for the strength of the current, a substantial leeway eastwards had set us ashore on a beach of the Ile de Seine.

1. Kapitän zur See Werner Fürbringer, summer 1938. In the inter-war period he was one of the pioneers who reconstructed the U-boat Arm.

2. *UB-2* at Borkum shortly before the run to Flanders in a near-hurricane, May 1915.

3. Hans Valentiner's *UB-16* seen from *UB-2* en route for the English coast, summer 1915.

4. Aft view of the *UB-2* conning tower with the boat flooded down: perched around the coaming (left to right) coxswain Becker, telegraphist Schepp, ERA Hausmann and Lt Fürbringer.

5. A dangerous job: repair work on the after casing.

6. *UB-39* crewmen pose for the camera while cleaning the 8.8-cm deck gun which bombarded Seaham, 12 July 1916.

7. A manifestation of deep gloom as North Sea fishermen look on from the foredeck of *UB-39* while their trawler is sunk. Afterwards Fürbringer put them into a lifeboat close inshore.

8. Conning tower damage after colliding with the keel of the sinking *Pronto*.

9. Lt Fürbringer at the centre of the *UB-39* crew after the *Pronto* voyage.

10. Lt Fürbringer (centre) with Hans Valentiner (left, inclining forward). One of the other two young officers is the *Pour le Merite* holder Hundius, (but unfortunately Fürbringer did not indicate which).

11. Korvettenkapitän Hans Bartenbach, CO of the U-Flotilla, Flanders, on the quayside at Bruges awaiting a returning U-boat. During the inter-war period he helped form the Argentine submarine force and eventually retired in the rank of Vice-Admiral.

12. A British sailing ship ablaze and down by the head.

13. Sunk! A freighter takes her death plunge.

.The *Clan Davidson* of Glasgow settling after being torpedoed by Fürbringer's *UC-17*. Once the crew were clear she was scuttled with explosives.

15. The waste of a torpedo on a prize, but necessary when an enemy destroyer appeared.

16. An hour ago a fine three-master on her lawful occasions, now a derelict, afire and left to her fate.

Chapter 9

LUCKY VOYAGE

At the end of the mission, I docked *UC-70* in the shipyard at Ostend and signed the boat over to the repairers, leaving the Chief Engineer and four men aboard as watchkeepers. The remainder of the complement took barracks leave at Bruges. It had not been possible to lay the boat up for repair there because of the long waiting list for the yards.

We made the best we could of the time in port with all its pleasures, the best of which was to have an undisturbed lie-in. On the first night ashore I celebrated my promotion but it was difficult to relax and shake off the accumulated tensions of the previous three weeks at sea. But once the feel of life ashore reasserted itself we made up for it, and then I slept like the proverbial log in those wonderfully comfortable Belgian four-poster beds.

British bomber aircraft came over almost every night and the German 15-cm AA guns which ringed the town of Bruges rent the dark skies with splinters of steel, their heavy salvoes shaking the very foundations of the barracks in which we slept. But this was insufficient to disturb the slumber of a U-boat man.

Drunk with sleep but subconsciously troubled I rolled back and forth across my mahogany double bed. I thought I had heard thunder in the distance, but was unsure if I had dreamed it.

"Herr Kapitänleutnant," a voice said insistently.

"What's up?" I cried, jumping out of my bed, ready to spring for the conning tower ladder. My steward Tiede stood at my bedside laughing. At last I remembered where I was.

"May it please the Kapitänleutnant to get up at once and proceed to Ostend with the Flotilla Commander. Monitors bombarded the coast at 0400 this morning. A 38-cm shell exploded in the harbour basin where *UC-70* was moored. Two steam trawlers, two lighters and our boat have been sunk."

"What happened to our men on watch?" I asked as I dressed hurriedly.

"Nobody was hurt. The two sentries left the boat and took shelter as soon as the firing began," Tiede told me.

A few minutes later a staff car conveyed the Flotilla Commander and me to Ostend. The small harbour was a pitiful sight with its crop of capsized auxiliary warships and our sunken *UC-70*, of which only the conning tower was above water. None of the caretaker crew had been wounded even though their shelter had taken a hit.

Although *UC-70* would be raised, it would take many months to restore her to an operational condition and the Navy could not afford to have a seasoned U-boat crew idle for months on end. Nevertheless, even the new boat for which I was listed would not be ready until the autumn of 1917, two or three months away. While the FdU, Korvettenkapitän Bartenbach, deliberated on how I should be employed in the interim, the commander of *UC-17* fell ill and I was ordered to replace him. Within a few days I was steering my new command for the western approaches to the English Channel.

This was at the crucial time when U-boats were working most feverishly. At all costs we knew we had to maintain against Allied merchant shipping the high success rates which were the prerequisite for an early conclusion to hostilities in Germany's favour. For what would become of Germany if we should fail? The spectre of this grim question overshadowed each of us. We discussed it often with the men, reassuring them repeatedly that we would eventually overcome the enemy Entente, and they were convinced.

However, the point in time was fast approaching by when in

the calculations of the Admiral Staff the U-boat Arm would have had to demonstrate beyond doubt a drastic reduction in the enemy's lines of supply from overseas. It had been part of their advocacy in 1916 for the policy of unrestricted submarine warfare that the heightened campaign would achieve its objective within six months. Five of these six months had now elapsed. Berlin was confident that the peoples of Britain and France were being forced to make the same sacrifices as those enforced upon Germany by the maritime blockade and that the Entente Cordiale would collapse before American aid became effective.

As to the fact that the prognostications of the Admiral Staff were based on the more simple comparisons of 1916, that the prosecution of the war had since then become more arduous and that British anti-submarine measures had improved by leaps and bounds Berlin remained silent. We U-boat men saw it as ominous that five months of unrestricted submarine warfare were already behind us and Berlin now thought that the end was near.

At the beginning of the six months officers at the Front believed that the period given was sufficient. Only at the end of five months did it begin to dawn upon us that, despite the huge inroads into enemy tonnage, the first half-year would not bring the desired conclusion to affairs. Why not? We had the sinkings statistics. By how much did the Admiral Staff's declaration of tonnage sunk exceed the true figure? We discussed this question endlessly in the mess. We knew the names of more than 50% of all ships sunk by the U-boat Arm. Knowing the names, we knew the registered tonnage. The error in the estimates therefore lay in the remaining 40% or so, but on the whole it was likely to be a diminishing error as U-boat commanders obtained more practice in estimating ship size. If the expected victory had not been achieved, the fault was not attributable to exaggerated estimates of tonnage sunk. So where?

U-boat commanders knew the answer by what they observed. We sank ship after ship, a fantastic number, and yet it always seemed to us that we were failing to make any impression on the numbers of merchant vessels putting into enemy ports.

Where were they all coming from? Was enemy shipping being better organized or had the Entente succeeded in chartering a much larger proportion of the world capacity than was considered possible by German naval planners? Probably both.

It was therefore in the high summer of 1917 that some of us began to suspect that we were not only faced with the task of destroying the merchant tonnage of the Entente nations, but that we were pitted in a gigantic battle against practically all the tonnage in the world. Actually we were not as clear on the matter as I have expressed it here, but certainly there was an awareness in the mind of veteran underwater seafarers who could compare what we found to be the case today with how it had been previously.

It was of course our duty to maintain the level of buoyant optimism which had been characteristic of unrestricted submarine warfare at its outset. In this we were assisted by the continuing descriptions made by our foreign agents as to the degree to which our sinkings were having their effect on the comforts of English life. But we saw what we saw, and in discussions between intimates the first doubts had begun to emerge about the possibility of victory. I must emphasize that only in the most intimate circles did these conversations take place, but they cast a long shadow.

At about the time I assumed command of *UC-17* I had become personally less optimistic about our final success. I recall a number of conversations with another commander who was a close friend of mine and who shared my scepticism. Of course, neither of us spoke of our inner doubts in the mess or to our subordinates, and outwardly we remained cheerfully optimistic. Moreover, we were young, and at sea we were seized by the passion of U-boat life, fired by the ambition of achieving, as a unit, something worthwhile towards the great vision of victory.

UC-17 had arrived in the operational area at the western end of the English Channel. After the first few days at sea it was clear that I had a good, reliable crew. We laid our mines and, to enable commander and crew to test their mettle, the gods of war sent along two sailing ships, a medium-sized ship flying the

90

red duster and a large American vessel, which we quickly "gobbled up". The latter had made every conceivable advance preparation for the contingency of being sunk, and no sooner than it takes to tell the boats were away, crammed with the crew and their belongings. I got a fright when in one of the lifeboats an engine was started up and the bows pointed towards us. This was something beyond my experience and I had the deck gun trained on the launch, at which the occupants raised their hands and called over that it was just a harmless lifeboat. This was absolutely true, the ingenious Americans having arranged to make it easy for themselves should their ship be sunk not too far offshore, when they would motor to the nearest coast independent of sail and oar. Every available square metre of their sailing vessel, including the upper deck, was stacked with oil in wooden barrels. Such a ship could not be sunk by explosive charges because even when the hull was immersed to the rails, she would still float on the cargo. Therefore she had to be set ablaze.

My prize crew of arsonists went across smartly to the doomed barque and within a few minutes thick smoke was rising from several places on deck. After half an hour the whole upper deck was in flames licking higher than the mastheads. This indicated that the destruction of the vessel could be claimed as certain without waiting to watch her sink and we could set off on the hunt for more pickings.

I set course to the south. Even hours later, looking astern, we could still see the enormous concentration of black smoke billowing out from the distant derelict, reminiscent of a volcanic eruption. It was evening before the last vestiges of the huge conflagration were finally extinguished.

A little later the starboard lookout forward reported the mastheads of a steamer below the horizon. The ship was bound almost directly towards us but then altered a shade so that we could see both masts. This was most convenient for our attack, since we had only to dive and wait for her to present her fore-ship for a torpedo.

I took the boat below as soon as the steamer appeared above the horizon and kept the ship under observation. It seemed a nice fat tub, very broad in the beam and deeply laden. I noticed two lookouts in the foremast crow's nest which meant I would have to exercise some caution in my use of the periscope. I hoped that we had not already been spotted while surfaced as this might be a ship's master who had learned by his mistakes! After reporting my observations into the control room, I noticed a quite different sort of tension among the men. Every U-boat man is happiest whenever the situation is not quite straightforward, when there is some kind of complication which has to be overcome first. This was straightforward. We were on course for the fat steamer, torpedo tube ready, nothing to it. I raised the periscope – and cursed.

"Full astern both!" The enemy freighter had changed course and was now well placed to ram us. I was forced to move out of her path and then turn quickly to prevent her escape. My new heading was facing 180 degrees about; the motors were hammering so furiously that the whole boat trembled; the vibrations were far worse in the tower than elsewhere. The din was appalling, and while this was going on the coxswain and I had to plot the new attack course and the firing angle. Our attention was fully concentrated on this task as everything depended on the accuracy of the calculations. To make ourselves heard we had to shout. Once the compass needle quivered at the correct heading, I took a peep through the periscope. It looked good. I fired the torpedo. It hit forward of midships.

On the deck of the stricken freighter panic erupted. I passed close by her stern and read off the name *Clan Davidson*, Glasgow. Being so near even though still submerged, I could see the reason for the mad excitement aboard the casualty. The crew were Lascars, maybe with no experienced seafarers among them, and their attempts to get the lifeboats lowered were almost hilarious. Fortunately for them the sea was relatively calm and the boats survived the maltreatment, finishing up afloat and the right way up. After a while these craft assembled well astern of the *Clan Davidson* and I surfaced among them, invited the captain aboard with the ship's papers and sent my prize crew off to speed up the sinking by means of a few explosive charges. From the ship's manifest I could see why the ship was taking so long to settle: she had a mixed cargo which included 3000 tons of butter which gave her a lot of buoyancy.

After setting the explosives the prize crew put back carrying, as a souvenir for me, the breech block from the steamer's 13-cm gun. The chunk of metal was so heavy that their return was delayed somewhat and they were still well short of being alongside when the three explosive charges went off. The sea rushed into the large engine-room and the steamer submerged quickly with a loud roar. It was a long way to the bottom. We had 3000 metres under the keel here, although the point did not interest us then, as our immediate priority was to search the captain's lifeboat thoroughly for hidden documents.

Suddenly – and we could hardly believe what we saw – eight to ten large barrels rocketed up from the depths one after another. Now we thought about the great depth here. A few seconds later we were thunderstruck to see a large sheep follow the barrels up. Mouths agape, we watched the animal get under way as if it were the most natural thing in the world to start pedalling for home after having been ejected to the surface by ten atmospheres of pressure.

My men on deck gave a great howl of joy, partly in expectation of a fat mutton roast, but also in admiration of the amazing performance of the brave old sheep. We made the effort to save him as if he were a man overboard. Just as he was about to go under for the last time we got a rope round his midriff. He was dreadfully breathless; possibly his lungs had burst as a result of his ascent from the deep. Quickly he was despatched, nimbly shorn of his fleece, which was thrown into the sea, and the edible remainder conveyed to the galley.

Meanwhile all five lifeboats of the *Clan Davidson* had made off to the east under lugsail. They were already little more than white dots in the distance when a steamer hove in sight in their general direction. This ship would have to be sunk too. To avoid detection I dived at once and approached under water. Through the periscope I watched the steamer change course towards the lifeboats. This might be fatal for what I had in mind. The proposed rescue took him well away from us.

Although the batteries were almost depleted of charge, I

decided nevertheless to head for the probable meeting point of steamer and lifeboats at full speed and below periscope depth. After ten minutes the boat rose for a brief look at periscope depth and I found my expectations confirmed by events. Well ahead, the steamer lay stopped in the water taking aboard the men from the first lifeboat. Three of the other boats were close to the ship, while the fifth was some distance off. I could see that my only opportunity for attack was when the steamer reached the fifth lifeboat, but even then it would be touch and go. Nevertheless I had to try.

I bore down on the fifth lifeboat. Everything depended on reaching the rendezvous no later than when the steamer arrived there. I was panting with the physical effort of operating the periscope; at speed the boat was pitching heavily and at the optic I had to move continually up and down the conning tower ladder to prevent the tip of the periscope from projecting too far above the waves, which might betray our presence to the steamer's lookouts. While we were still beyond torpedo range the little sailing lifeboat neared the steamer and disappeared on her lee side from where the lifeboat's occupants would board the rescuing ship. This would have its advantages for us, however, in that the attention of the steamer's crew and lookouts would be distracted away from the windward side, where we were making our rapid and stealthy approach.

For a moment while the periscope was retracted I reflected on the morality of the impending situation. On the one hand, the honourable seamen on that ship, true to the highest traditions of their calling, had willingly placed their lives in the greatest danger to save the shipwrecked of the *Clan Davidson*. And all the thanks they were going to get for it was a German torpedo. On the other hand, I remembered the misery of the German Home Front, with our people reduced to starvation level by a merciless naval blockade, and I thought too of the enormous struggle in which Germany was engaged for her very existence. All the Allied freighters we saw out here, every single one of them, were ostensibly proceeding as if on their lawful peacetime occasions, but in reality they stood shoulder to shoulder committed to the defeat of Germany, and they all carried materials for use in the war against Germany. This latter was the argument which had to carry weight with me: these ships had to be sunk inevitably, relentlessly, unsparingly. That much we owed to the German people, even if as seamen we did it with a heavy heart.

I raised the periscope. We were at the limit of our range, a kilometre – our so-called "war-torpedoes" would run for only 1000 metres – but the steamer had had time to complete the rescue operation. She was still stopped in the water, but could set off at any moment, and if she did so while the torpedo was running, it would miss. I decided to fire at once, aiming forward of midships. My splendid watch officer, Achilles, stood at my side with a stopwatch counting off each hundred metres of the torpedo's run. The time was too long. I had missed. Then at 900 metres a shock wave rocked the boat. Up periscope! The column of water thrown up by the explosion against the ship's side was still in the act of collapsing.

On the steamer confusion reigned. Then some form of order was restored, boat after boat was let down and manned, including those of the *Clan Davidson* so recently heaved up, and finally there were nine lifeboats drifting around the stricken freighter. I waited fifteen minutes and, as the steamer showed no inclination to take the final plunge, I surfaced and from 100 metres range the gun crew fired a few 8.8-cm shells at her waterline.

The derelict began to settle a little faster but as I left the scene with a westwards heading a destroyer, apparently an American, was seen coming up from the south at high speed. Dive! Once below the Chief Engineer told me that the batteries were almost drained and we would have to proceed at our lowest revolutions to conserve what was left. This was worrying, for the destroyer was rapidly approaching overhead and we had come little distance from the spot where we had submerged. A series of depth charges dropped into that patch would be decidedly unpleasant for us. His propellers were thrashing ever closer; all report centres had advised of them; suddenly a single depth charge exploded very close with a great blast. It was the only one. Perhaps he had now run out of them.

The destroyer was manoeuvring, and we could hear various screw noises, but there was no fresh attack. I risked a peep at periscope depth after it fell reasonably quiet; the destroyer was slowly patrolling the area where the steamer had just sunk. It was almost dusk before I judged it safe to surface but scarcely were we under way than the lookouts reported the masts and funnel of a steamer steering NE and coming up from the west. With four masts this would be a big ship. The hull was still below the horizon. I called down for full ahead both diesels, high speed being necessary to close the gap between us before night fell when we would lose him to sight. It was going to be a mighty struggle to keep up, and before even starting we had to recharge the batteries, for if we did not do so and had to dive unexpectedly during the pursuit, it would be problematical.

Once ready to set off, I asked the engine-room for the highest output, and they gave it all they had. Such a pursuit as this one demanded and got the best out of all individuals aboard a U-boat, since it was a change from the deadening and endless monotony of routine cruising in a sealed tube. Already I had personally spent a day in gymnastics at the periscope and, in spite of the exertions of the crewmen, their faces were grubby, but beaming and alive.

I kept the large enemy freighter under close observation to determine whether he was steaming a direct course or zig-zagging across it. If the latter was the case, our task was doubly difficult. I had to plot an interception course so precise as to place my U-boat ahead of the freighter's bows for a simple kill in the darkness. If he was making irregular zigzags the success of my navigation would be more luck than skill. Chance favoured our losing the steamer permanently in the darkness, that much I knew. In the end, a great disappointment probably awaited us, but one still had to try.

Night fell swiftly and the steamer was lost to sight. How much we would give for infra-red vision! I cautioned the look-outs, "Take it easy. Don't strain with your eyes. We're not likely to spot the target for another three-quarters of an hour yet." By then we would have reached his mean course, and our binoculars would never fall until we had him for sure.

After forty-five minutes the bows turned along the mean course of the steamer, although of the latter there was no sign. I reduced speed and stared astern. I was sure he would come up on us from our rear.

"Shadow ahead to starboard," the boatswain reported. A glance through my binoculars confirmed this as our steamer. I cursed; he had sailed past us. A spurt at full speed proved only that he was faster. My only hope of arriving in the torpedo attack position was to race ahead on his true course while he wasted time making zigzags across it. I gave the orders and watched him vanish into the darkness.

Boys, I thought, this is the crunch, let's pray that the sixth sense we have had guiding us all day doesn't desert us now. We hammered onwards for twenty minutes, the lookouts wound up like clock-springs. I had the stern tube readied to fire our last torpedo. From whichever direction the steamer might next appear, I could now fire at once. A dark shadow appeared on the starboard quarter. He was too far away and the angle too acute for a stern shot. I would have to turn towards him, cross his "T" and then shoot from his starboard side. The steamer was emerging from the blackness, becoming ever more distinct. Already I could see the luminous great curves of white foam curling either side of his stem and I still hadn't crossed his "T". I was very uneasy and had devised my collision-avoidance tactic. A mistake was likely to be our last.

In moments of high tension time often slows, for it is a product of perception. At last we were crawling across the steamer's path. He was very close. A slight course adjustment convinced me he had seen us and was angling to ram. I was about to shout an emergency change of course to the helmsman when I saw the starboard side of the steamer at last. Now it was a question of what was loosed off first – the steamer's gun or my torpedo.

I had sent the lookouts below to diving stations and retained only the helmsman with me on the bridge. Aboard the ship I watched a lantern being run towards the poop to where the anti-submarine cannon would be fitted. But quickly! Another second or so and we will see who is the winner!

"Torpedo los!" The shining missile roared from its tube. I counted off the painfully long seconds as the torpedo ran. I expected the steamer to open fire on us within a half minute. Time was up; the torpedo must have missed. I ordered the helmsman below and had my hands on the hatch cover to follow him, but I took a last glance at the steamer and at that moment saw a huge column of water rear up aft where the torpedo had struck. It had certainly taken its time getting there, I thought. Our determination and effort had paid off. The steamer began to settle and once the sea was lapping across the after holds I steered *UC-17* round his stern and came upon the knot of lifeboats which I summoned alongside. As the survivors had no provisions I handed them down some bread and water, although we were short of both ourselves. The steamer was the *Monarque*. The voice of the mate shouted from one of the boats, "It's a pity you hit us first!" Then he explained that he had seen the U-boat as we crossed the freighter's bow. He had grabbed a lantern from the bridge and sprinted to the gun on the poop deck. Just when it had been reported clear to fire our torpedo had hit and rendered the gun unserviceable.

With a wave we parted from the lifeboats. The night was dark, the coast was far, the war was hard and unsparing. Long after midnight the off-watch men slumped into their bunks. I remained on the bridge, staring into the darkness until the dawn broke slowly in the east. I was tense with the stress and excitement and sleep was far from my thoughts. I had ordered a course for home, our mines having been laid and all our torpedoes fired off. Finally, hours later, in a state of growing exhaustion, I dragged myself below and fell into the sleep of the dead.

Scarcely a few seconds seemed to have elapsed when I heard an excited commotion on the conning tower. Cursing in annoyance I went up to the bridge. It was midday and the sun beamed down from almost overhead. I was blinded by the brightness of the light. Incredible that what had seemed a brief, deep doze for only a few seconds had been in reality many hours, but after the events of the previous day it was little wonder.

"Sailing ship two points to starboard," the coxswain reported. Several brilliant white sails graced the horizon. An hour later the large American schooner *Calena* was on the seabed. She had been bound for North America from France in ballast. Her crew of blacks, all wearing white industrial gloves, were soon heading for the French coast under lugsail in their lifeboats.

A few days later *UC-17* put in at Bruges without further incident. Our tally for the voyage was 24,000 tons. We were heartily congratulated on such a brief but successful mission.

I made one further voyage in *UC-17*. Generally it went smoothly except for two minor incidents. West of Brest we torpedoed the British steamer *City of Florence*. The ship remained afloat and I sent a prize crew across to hasten her demise with a couple of explosive charges. The men took so long about it that I allowed *UC-17* to drift up closer for the purpose of enquiring into the reason for the delay. Suddenly there were four or five pistol shots in quick succession from inside the steamer. Naturally the worst scenario sprang to mind. I gave the recall signal on the battery whistle and at the same moment my three men appeared on deck through the doorway to the crew quarters in the fo'c'sle. Two were carrying a body between them.

"Do you need help?" I shouted in alarm through the megaphone.

"Thank you, no, Herr Kapitänleutnant," the watch officer roared back, grinning. "We can get this fat mutton over by ourselves!" and with these words the dead sheep was unceremoniously heaved over the railings into the dinghy below. The animal had been left aboard when the ship's crew abandoned their vessel. No explanation was offered as to why five shots had been required to despatch the sheep. The prize crew also brought me from the ship's deck a hand-sized fragment of the torpedo which had hit the doomed *City of Florence*. This was a rare souvenir of great value to a U-boat commander.

We had bad weather for our return, which was to our advantage for the passage of the Straits of Dover, and once through the British barrier we encountered calm sea conditions for the run in. It was about midday, *UC-17* was off the Belgian coast, quietly making for Zeebrügge.

"Port beam 200 metres a string of net buoys!" the watch officer shouted suddenly.

With a watchful eye I maintained our course parallel to this obstruction for a while, and then another string of buoys was seen bobbing to starboard, and I had to weave through them carefully. When a further set materialized ahead on the starboard hand I was forced to turn back, but now I could no longer find the access channel. We were hemmed in on all sides!

Net buoys were large glass balls supporting the headline of a long net of steel meshes to which a mine was attached at fifty metres intervals at a depth of about two metres. An insulating wire from each mine was connected to a battery on the hawser at the surface.

We were in a very difficult situation. I had stopped the boat and, while discussing the problem with the watch officer and coxswain, a part of the net, which was apparently drifting free, scraped alongside. As our feverish search for a gap proved unsuccessful, we were left with no alternative but to attempt to force a way through before we became entrammelled. But on which side should the attempt be made: where was the danger less?

The principle behind the net was fiendishly simple. As a U-boat charged through, the section of net broke away from the adjoining sections either side and wrapped itself around the boat, entangling in the propellers to bring the submarine to a standstill, while the mines came into contact with the outer hull and exploded. We knew these dangers well enough. Time was pressing, the situation grew more deadly with each passing minute. Our only hope was that the net would not function as designed.

Just as the engines burst into life, the watch officer pointed out a short stretch of net without batteries on the surface wire. Putting the helm hard over I made for it in the hope that the mines there would be inoperative. A few metres before the bows touched the net I cut the engines so as to drift down on the top wire with the propellors stopped to prevent tangling.

This was the moment of greatest tension. Would the sharp prow of the U-boat cut through the steel mesh, or would the net seize us like the tentacles of a giant octopus? On the bridge all eyes were riveted to the approaching net. Our bow touched. Curses! Was it beginning to wrap? No! Now the oblique prow rode over the headline, forcing it down. We were over. The hull was as smooth as an eel, with no projections on which a net could snag until it reached the propellors, but suddenly we were clear, the whole "mixed salad" behind us. I had the engines thrown to full ahead to get us safely to Bruges before midnight.

At 2100 hrs I called in at Zeebrugge to inform Flotilla by telephone of my arrival and an hour later, in total darkness, I inched the submarine through the narrow confines of Bruges harbour past torpedo-boats, small floating docks and lighters to moor alongside the quay wall. Once I stepped ashore, the mission was concluded officially. Each crewman tucked his few belongings under one arm and made off to the barracks building nearby where everything had been prepared for the homecoming. Here he could scrub off the accumulated filth of fourteen days or three weeks at sea in a U-boat and then sleep his fill in a comfortable, clean bed.

We officers trooped off as we were, unshaved, filthy, in greasy U-boat gear impregnated with every U-boat stink, and headed for the officers' mess in the centre of town. It was virtually Holy Writ to report on the mission to the Flotilla Commander in the original sartorial state on docking, following which we would then go to the mess, if we had arrived at night, to celebrate our safe return with comrades old and new.

My watch officer said he had something to sort out at the barracks and so I set off for the officers' mess alone, pounding through the silent streets of late-night Bruges in heavy seaboots with wooden soles. Clad in the thick U-boat gear one felt so disinclined to shed, I was soon sweating like a polar bear in the Sahara. Worse still, I had not yet reaccustomed myself to walking. At sea one strolled a U-boat's deck only in the finest weather and far from the enemy's shore. As both were rarities, one exercised by shifting weight from one foot to the other rather in the manner of the maribou. Thus I was close to

101

exhaustion when I arrived at the officers' mess. I found the street doors open and went up a short flight of marble steps into the corridor which led to the mess halls. There seemed a distinct lack of activity within. The bar was shuttered, which was a great pity since I could easily have sunk a litre bottle of beer forthwith. I knew that the Flotilla Commander would be in his office and I made a few improvements to my appearance in the washroom, pulling my scarf across my throat, raising the neck of my sweater high to hide the filthy shirt I had on. My hair was matted and unkempt and I combed it across with my fingers after scrubbing furiously at the nails for several minutes. Finally, I made another adjustment to the red peasant-kerchief I was never without. The Flotilla Commander could expect no better than this. I took a deep breath, strode to his chambers, threw open the door, took in those present with a single glance, recoiled in horror, made a deep bow, and closed the door firmly on my exit.

What a dirty trick! At Zeebrugge I had personally phoned news of my boat's return and no mention had been made then that Großadmiral Prince Heinrich von Preussen, General Inspector of the Navy and C-in-C Baltic Forces, was a guest of the officers' mess. What must His Highness have thought as I made my entrance still dressed in my pig's get-up? In a rage I tore off the scarf and stinking jacket as I stormed towards the washroom once more, but heard the door open from within and enticing voices summoning me, "Fips! Fips! Come back!" The Prince himself stood in the doorway, offering me his hand. "What's this, Fürbringer, making off as soon as you saw me? I should take a poor view of something like that!" And now he made me sit with him and recount the events of my latest mission in the minutest detail, followed by a summary of all my previous voyages. He wanted to hear everything, to hear about the crews, and to know by name those who had in some way distinguished themselves on operations. Meanwhile I was permitted to smoke only from the Prince's personal cigarette case, and he reserved to himself alone the right to refill my punch glass whenever it was empty. Thus we all fell under the irresistible charm of Prince Heinrich, revered in the Imperial

Navy as a nobleman in the highest sense of the word. He had a way of making one feel a hero, even though one realized his intention was to honour equally every U-boat man who knew the hard life of the Front.

The Prince remained with us until midnight, a seaman amongst seamen, and took his leave after making a short address of simple sincerity. He left a lasting impression of his natural majesty.

Chapter 10

DOVER–CALAIS

In the late summer of 1917, a few months after the visit of Prince Heinrich, I went to Bremen to commission my long-promised boat *UB-58*, proceeding then to Kiel to work-up and finally bringing the boat round the coast to Flanders. My wife, whom I had married in December 1916, came to Bremen to be with me. But far too swiftly for young love the time swept past. On the seas Germany's need was more urgent than ever; the huge gaps torn in our numbers had to be filled, and quickly.

Thus we soon had to part, and the little wife had to grit her teeth and be brave. Full of great hopes for my new command, I sailed down to Flanders. In the U-boat mess at Bruges there was the usual confident outlook, the undaunted aggressive spirit, the exuberant humour. The number of mess members had remained unchanged, only the faces were different. Many dear old faces were missing, many newer faces, scarcely remembered, had gone, never to reappear. But that was something which would only be apparent to somebody long absent from the mess. One came to terms with the inevitable and soon slipped back into the old carefree attitude. Reality and work demanded the whole man; there could be no place for gloomy imaginings of impending doom and destruction.

After a few days in port I took *UB-58* into the English Channel. Westwards of the Dover–Calais barrage one of the electric motors flooded. The engineer discovered a dangerous construction fault. As the same failure was likely to occur sooner or later in the other E-motors I terminated the mission and retired to Bruges. Fortunately the repairs could be made relatively quickly and, armed with the completion docket, I set out afresh for the English coast. But we were under the influence of a baleful star. This time it was the torpedoes. On several occasions I missed with shots that ought to have been certain hits. No explanation could be found for my apparent failure. Having achieved nothing approaching our expectations I slunk home.

On the next operation the torpedoes let me down again with a series of inexplicable misses. I obtained the proof I needed when I made an underwater attack on a steamer. Everything was favourable for us. The attack was carefully planned. The torpedo hissed out of the tube. The waves were capped by small white crests as far as the eye could see, and after firing I kept the periscope raised since there was no likelihood that the steamer's lookouts would spot it in the conditions. Many seconds earlier than when the torpedo should have hit the steamer there was a tremendous explosion. In the boat, light bulbs cracked, delicate instruments broke down. I watched the steamer continue its voyage, her master's alarm at the subterranean roar being evident by the huge change in his ship's heading and the alacrity with which he now left the scene.

It was clear that after leaving the tube my torpedo had headed straight for the bottom where it exploded, and unquestionably we were fortunate to have a few thousand metres below the keel: in the shallows the blast would probably have sunk us.

I had had great confidence in the torpedoes which had brought me success in the past. The recent sequence of failures was something quite new. I had introduced no innovations into my attack procedure and I was therefore convinced that the torpedoes were faulty.

Towards the end of the previous mission I had had two inexplicable misses and for that reason had returned to port prematurely, bringing home two unexpended torpedoes for workshop inspection. Shortly before leaving for the present operation I had been informed that the checked torpedoes were faultless. I refused to believe this and resolved not to allow the report to shake my self-confidence, for naturally a doubt now lurked. Towards the end of this indifferent voyage I still had a single torpedo. I had no confidence in it and my immediate impulse was to head for home. This was not possible, however, for every ship sunk edged Germany that much closer to salvation. The torpedo had to be found a billet.

I surfaced just before dusk. Whilst submerged I had had the mechanics completely overhaul the last torpedo and all working parts were reported in perfect order. Therefore it should run true.

We stood off the English coast between Portland and the Isle of Wight. Here one could occasionally find the odd ship close in. The night was not too dark and visibility was relatively good. We hung around for three hours and then fortune smiled upon us in the shape of a steamer heading westwards. We took up station parallel to this ship about two kilometres to seaward and made an accurate estimation of his speed and course. Then, from a position off his bow, I turned towards him for the attack and closed in using the electric motors at full speed to reduce the chance of being detected prematurely in the calm conditions. The approach ran off smoothly, just as if it were a peacetime exercise. I fired from 400 metres and the torpedo gurgled from the tube. Five seconds later there was a dull explosion underwater and it seemed as if the boat was lifted out of the water bodily by some giant's hand. I was deluged by damage reports from the conning tower, control-room and engine-room; it appeared that the rudder motor and both auxiliary and main engine plant were out of commission.

"Helm to manual control!" I shouted. This would take time. I was staring at the steamer. Although deprived of propulsion, we continued to make way through the water on a collision course for the target. Without screws or rudder we had no means of steering our way out of trouble. Fifty metres to go and we would hit the freighter abaft the beam. The ship had picked us out and opened fire with her stern gun but we were so close that the barrel couldn't be depressed sufficiently to hit us and the shells roared harmlessly overhead.

Just a few seconds before we would have collided the helmsman got the rudder working manually and the boat sheered under the counter of the merchantman with less than two metres to spare. Now I had to reduce our profile to the minimum for when we came into the field of fire of his gun. I turned to him stern-to. The steamer let us have a few more desultory rounds, but the plumes of water which reared up where the shells hit indicated such wild inaccuracy that I felt relatively untroubled as the boat slowed to a standstill. But now we had to work fast to get the engines back in working order. In her present state the boat could not submerge. For the time being we were adrift and helpless in the enemy's inshore waters. The sharpest watch was necessary to give me the best possible chance of preserving life if I had to scuttle the boat and so I posted the lookouts with the keenest vision on the conning tower. I stood on the bridge, and once I was assured that everything necessary had been taken in hand I broke into a tirade of such vehemence and bitterness that the crew who heard it must have wondered about my mental condition.

The depth of the seabed had been 25 metres, and so the torpedo went off about 20 metres below the keel. Presumably this had happened some distance dead ahead, otherwise the boat would have been blown to pieces. I would certainly have a few strong comments to make on the subject to the torpedo engineers in Bruges when I got there. It was a source of constant wonder to me how divine providence was always on hand to ensure my personal survival of every disaster and breakdown.

That same night propulsion and diveability were fully restored. Some damage was beyond repair with the tools available on board, but initially this did not cause a problem. The batteries forward were in a particularly bad way, most of the cells being cracked, and sulphuric acid, which corrodes iron very quickly, was on the flooring of the pressure hull. The urgency of our return could not now be overstated!

By day I steered a northerly mid-Channel course and timed for dusk our arrival at the Dover–Calais nets which I proposed to navigate in darkness. Shortly before nightfall we came up in

107

the vicinity of several destroyers – a sure sign that we were close to the barrier – and submerged.

By the time I judged it safe to surface it was dark; but what was this ahead? The boat was bathed in the harsh glare of five or six huge searchlights trained on us from the direction in which the net barrier lay. I assumed that this was some kind of special operation and decided to wait until it was over. As time passed I realized that the great beams of light had no other purpose than to illuminate the area. This was something new – a searchlight barrier. But what was it intended to achieve? The obvious conclusion was that the British wanted us to run submerged to elude the light barrier because they had set up some ghastly new trap below. I have to admit that I felt none too happy as I contemplated attempting to slip blindfold through an unknown sunken obstruction designed to kill me.

How was it to be achieved? In a heavy swell a breakthrough on the surface could usually be risked, for the boat would be rarely visible, not even in the searchlight beams, but tonight the sea was almost calm. I had no choice but to do what the English wanted and submerge, but I would not do them the favour of going deep as they obviously wished. I would trim the boat as close to the surface as I could and allow nothing to force me deeper, navigating neatly between the patrol boats above and the minefield below.

We set off on the surface for the searchlight barrier, not diving until blinded in the glare. I trimmed the boat so that the keel was thirteen metres below the surface, the highest point of the conning tower then being five metres below the surface. This ensured that a destroyer could pass overhead without colliding with the tower, but as a merchant steamer usually drew from six to eight metres fully laden and would demolish the tower if crossing above us, I brought the helmsman down to the steering position in the control room and sealed off the tower at the lower hatch. If we were rammed, the tower would take the force but the rest of the boat would probably survive undamaged.

We now crept submerged through the area in which the barrier proper protecting the Folkestone–Boulogne merchant traffic was rigged. I knew there were bound to be mines here moored below eight metres where they were harmless to steamers but lethal to U-boats and I was conscious of the need to maintain the shallowest possible depth.

There was great tension among the men; no word was spoken. They all knew how dangerous our situation was. The silence was broken only by the hum of the electric motors and now and again the rattle of the rudder machinery. Twice propeller noises were heard in the vicinity and reported in a whisper from various centres to the control room. The tension increased, we were coiled in readiness, but then the noises slowly dwindled.

Finally by my reckoning we were directly before the barrier. Here the mines would definitely be set shallow and we would have to hang only inches below the surface. I trimmed the boat at eight metres so that the bridge was almost breaking through. Now came the ticklish part.

I raised the periscope half a metre above the surface. It was bathed in light and I could see nothing. After a while I got used to the glare and managed to pick out where the searchlight ships were adrift. One was stationed on my starboard hand and I saw that we would have to pass him very close. I altered course to give this vessel more sea room to starboard. The motors were running full out and the distance to the leading ship diminished rapidly. For a few seconds the searchlight was trained away from us and I saw the contours of a large destroyer. He was still 300 metres ahead when we escaped from the cone of his searchlight and I had the opportunity to study his outline. While I was doing this, however, he changed course and bore down on us suddenly, the beam shining directly into my periscope eye. Had he seen us? Was he about to ram? In the light I could not see him, and I had been so cautious with the periscope that I doubted if he could have detected it, but he might have heard our motors. I retracted the tube gingerly, whispered for the motors to be put at minimum revolutions, the helm hard to port. At any moment he might go for the ramming manoeuvre, but it was preferable to run the risk than go deeper instead. The grinding of the destroyer's propellors grew louder, but after listening for some time we decided that his engines were at slow ahead, and soon he turned away. There had been nothing significant in his course changes and we breathed a sigh of relief.

Nevertheless the British naval concentration must have known that we were about, for no sooner had we left the first bag of tricks astern than another presented itself. Behind the line of searchlight destroyers the night was suddenly illuminated bright as day when a group of patrol vessels fired star shell simultaneously. Every detail of the sea surface was visible. These latter vessels were doubtless blinded by their own pyrotechnics and were a matter of no concern to us; our worry was the more distant warships which we suspected would be closely examining the backcloth of light for the outline of enemy submarines. I remained submerged, if only just.

Once again we were in an abysmal situation. Below us the mines, astern a sea of light and a background against which our silhouette would be immediately visible should we be incautious enough to surface; ahead the impenetrable darkness in which more ugly surprises were undoubtedly lurking.

About twenty minutes after passing the searchlight battery a large destroyer crossed our wash on a course parallel to the brightness. This would be one of the distant observers waiting to pounce on any U-boat unwary enough to be surfaced after having emerged from the lit area. I blessed my lucky star that I had read the situation correctly and remained submerged.

Fifteen minutes later I judged it safe to come up. The boat surfaced and ran towards Ostend at full speed. It felt as if she had picked up the smell of home. A cross on the chart told me that we had reached the point of safety at which it was my custom to invite the Chief Engineer and Watchkeeping Officer to join me in the mess for a few minutes to celebrate our success with a glass of port.

It was 0500 hrs. I was dog-tired, the night was still pitch-black and after all the harum-scarum of the early hours we felt we could now relax a little. With a yawn I had just told Tiede, my steward, to break open the port when the boatswain of the watch called down, "Warship on starboard beam heading straight for us!"

I raced to the bridge, quickly sized up the approaching vessel,

110

now so close that neither a crash dive nor an avoiding manoeuvre could save us. We were at his mercy. Our only chance was to ram him at full speed before he could strike us, and at whatever cost!

"Both engines maximum speed ahead, helm to starboard!" I screamed down the tower in great excitement.

The officer of the watch, Leutnant Otto, who had continued to observe the oncoming vessel, remarked calmly, "Herr Kapitänleutnant, I don't think we need to ram him. He may not be coming for us after all." The helm was still hard over in the development of the ramming manoeuvre. I realized that my officer was right. At once I had the boat's head turned directly to face the enemy ship and reversed engines. This presented our narrowest silhouette to the recipient of our attentions, which had been, however, unaware of our existence throughout this alarming few minutes.

Once the enemy warship was well astern I opened the bottle of port and drank a toast, not to the conclusion of the mission, but to the wide-awake young Otto who had saved the boat. The boatswain and I had both made an erroneous assumption, while Otto had remained cool under pressure and judged the situation correctly.

I found rest impossible below and watched the dawn from the bridge. Then we had to dive, for in these Belgian coastal waters there lurked many British submarines. Their purpose was to take the lives of their German colleagues just when the latter, tired and worn down from the stresses of a long mission, arrived off the coast of Flanders and, believing themselves safe home, were thus keeping a less keen lookout than they should. In this manner many gaps had been chiselled in our ranks. Most of us who survived made it a principle to remain submerged by day.

I put UB-58 down on the seabed and allowed all free hands a long sleep. At dusk we surfaced and a little after midnight moored alongside the quay at Bruges.

Early next morning I strode to the torpedo workshop for a row with them about my two bottom runners, but before I could open my mouth the supervisor came towards me waving a sheaf of notes. "Good news, Herr Kapitänleutnant. Just before you sailed I wrote to the torpedo factory at Friedrichsort about your faulty torpedoes. They examined the K-torpedo and you are quite right, there is a construction fault in the depth plate which would either cause the torpedo to head for the bottom or develop other depth-keeping irregularities. The fault is now being rectified in all the remaining torpedoes of this type!"

It had certainly taken enough time to locate this malfunction, and for me it was too much time. The torpedo failures of the two previous missions had brought me to the verge of nervous exhaustion, and when I requested a leave of convalescence it was granted immediately.

My crew was given leave but remained at the disposition of the Flotilla because the repairs to the boat were fairly major.

Two days later I reported for a course of treatment at the Harzburg military hospital. It was 18 February 1918. It was raining and cold, the heating in my hotel was feeble, the catering poor and the fare scanty. Nevertheless after a few days I felt much improved and had regained my enthusiasm for seafaring. It came as a hammer-blow on the tenth day of my recuperation to be informed in a letter from U-Flotilla Admiral Staff Officer II that *UB-58* had put out into the Channel two days previously under a new commander. None of the listed repairs had been carried out to the corroding boat. They had been postponed until her return. My convalescence had been considered essential and for this reason I had not been recalled from sickness leave. Instead I was to report to Hamburg in fourteen days to commission a new boat.

After reading this letter I sank down sick at heart. I felt that somebody had stolen my boat and kidnapped the crew. I had brought at least half of them with me from the previous boats I had commanded and I felt a personal responsibility for each man. It seemed an act akin to betrayal that they should have been committed into strange hands on my behalf. I was appalled at the decision of U-Flotilla, for I would have returned at once to Bruges to resume command had I been invited to do so. And I had even lost my steward, the most loyal man I had ever known, Matrose Tiede, whom I had dragged with me from boat

112

to boat from the very beginning, who had become engaged and then married on the same day as I, and who always had a ready smile no matter what his preoccupation might be.

It did not bear thinking that I might lose all these people at a stroke, never sail in the future with a single one of them. I wrote a strongly worded letter of protest to U-Flotilla and received a mild rebuke in reply.

Inwardly I knew for certain from the moment when I read the first letter that *UB-58* would not return from this patrol. Three weeks later U-Flotilla wrote to tell me that *UB-58* was missing, believed lost with all hands, and I felt a part of me die.

Chapter 11

RAMMED!

I commissioned my new boat *UB-110* at the Blohm & Voss shipyard, Hamburg, and, after successful completion of trials and working-up, sailed her round the Dutch coast to Flanders. During this delivery voyage the port diesel broke down. As usual there was no capacity in the Bruges yard and I received orders to take the boat to Ostend to have the engine attended to.

It was a day in late June when we went, oppressively humid, the air calm, the type of day when the landsman is forever waving away bothersome flies. It was excellent flying weather, and the diligent U-boat commander knew from experience that he must be alert for unwelcome aviators.

UB-110 had left Zeebrugge for the one-hour run to Ostend and was standing about 2 kilometres offshore. The boat was cleared for an emergency dive but I had installed a machine gun on the upper casing and manned the quick-loading anti-aircraft gun. We had covered about half the distance when the aft lookout reported two aircraft coming in from the sea towards the coast. It was assumed that these would be German aircraft returning from a reconnaissance flight, but I decided to have recognition flares loaded and ready, but only fire them off if the planes should approach.

They turned towards us! Surely they didn't think we were

English? My new watch officer, Tietze, allayed my fears. It was a German type, he informed me.

"Fair enough," I said, "but I think I'll still give the aircraft alarm, all the same."

Scarcely had I done so than both aircraft lost altitude from 600 to 150 metres and headed for us in no uncertain manner. And then at last we saw the blue-white-red roundels on the fuselage.

"Open fire!" I shouted and at once all buttonholes spewed flame and lead. I put the helm hard to starboard and ordered maximum speed. The boat described a large circle. This put the first pilot off his aim and he decided to bomb. A few seconds later he dropped a large dustbin and this looked so comical that we all burst into laughter. When the bomb exploded thirty metres away the blast was so horrendous that we no longer saw the funny side after all.

The pilot banked and made a second bombing run. Another dustbin fell while *UB-110* weaved this way and that. The bomb exploded ten metres away. This seemed to empty his bomb-bays but before I had the opportunity to congratulate myself his rear-gunner spattered my iron deck with a fierce and accurate stream of bullets. At the same time the companion aircraft roared in. The helm was being spun madly from side to side to spoil the aim: it was our only defence since the machine gun had ceased to function after the first few rounds. Our manoeuvring seemed to confuse the second pilot and his first dustbin exploded well wide, but to make amends the next was so close that the whole boat trembled like a struck gong. The rear-gunner's virtuosity was impressively accurate, but the five-man bridge watch was in no danger, since we had already made a hasty descent into the conning tower for shelter. From there we heard the bullets spraying the upper deck, but this was soon replaced by the sharp crack of land-based anti-aircraft artillery.

We remanned the bridge and saw stabs of lightning from all along the coast. The guns sowed the sky with white puffs of cloud wherever a shell exploded; the two aircraft were already heading for home. It was a pity that the coastal batteries had reacted so promptly to the alert; the two aircraft were almost within range of the coastal forts during the attack and another few seconds would have exposed them to the heavy concentrated fire of many calibres.

On 3 July 1918 I received orders to proceed with *UB-110* to the English coast that night. It was the boat's first operational mission. I am not really superstitious but I now remember as curiously significant my parting conversation with the FdU Flanders, Korvettenkapitän Bartenbach. On numerous occasions I had dwelt at sea far longer than the FdU approved, even though I had always brought boat and crew safely home eventually despite all the breakdowns and malfunctions which were usually the cause of my delayed return. As I reported *UB-110* ready to sail on this new mission, he took his leave of me with the words, "Do me a special favour, Fürbringer and don't stay out so long this time!" He held my hand long in his as though he knew that I would not return.

I put on my U-boat combinations and heavy sea boots, clambered aboard *UB-110* and cast off. We negotiated the Bruges Canal in pitch darkness. Near Zeebrugge my watch officer, Leutnant Tietze, reported, "Herr Kapitänleutnant, the cook has forgotten all the cutlery. What should we do now?"

I knew what I would like to have done now. First I assembled the catering Petty Officer and cook and gave them a dressing down probably without equal in their careers. Obviously there could be no question of going back for the knives and forks, or when the story got around we would be the laughing stock of the U-boat Arm. The problem had to be solved unobtrusively. Meanwhile we had entered the chamber of the lock at Zeebrugge, and there we pressured the lock-keeper into letting us have his entire reserve stock of eating utensils, which was enough for half the crew. He had second thoughts a short while afterwards and jumped aboard the casing to plead, "Please be sure to bring them back." I gave him my promise and a bag of money to defray the costs, should they be lost.

We put out from Zeebrugge and arrived without mishap two days later off the English east coast town of Hartlepool, my assigned sea area of operations.

116

By July 1918 it had become extremely difficult for a U-boat to get in an attack. The British massed their merchant ships in well-protected large convoys which they sailed down this coast irregularly, seldom and close inshore. If a U-boat missed a convoy, the commander would have to hang around for days for the next one to present itself. Precious time was being lost in doing so.

In the last twelve months the British had made unbelievable strides towards improving their anti-submarine defences. The convoy system had proved itself beyond all expectations. Their depth charges were packed with more explosive. They had perfected a mine copied from the German model. They had put into service much improved underwater listening devices. These were all developments which made the work of the U-boat commander more difficult and reduced his chances of success and survival. In the month of May 1918, the Entente succeeded for the first time in launching more tonnage than the U-boats destroyed.

Accordingly we were no longer convinced that the U-boat alone was capable of bringing about the decisive change in our fortunes. The enormous opportunity which unrestricted submarine warfare had provided us with had been visibly reduced, while the importance of the U-boat for the policymakers had, if anything, increased.

In the west the German armies were on the offensive. On three occasions since 18 March 1918 they had attempted to breach the Allied lines. Again and again they concentrated their full strength in a desperate effort to swing the land war in Germany's favour and we, the U-boat Arm, were their right flank in this enormous struggle. We too gave our all for victory. It was more urgent than ever; every single ton sunk counted.

For every ton the U-boats sent to the bottom in this last and most gruelling year of the Great War we had to fight more bitterly than ever before. We had sunk our teeth into the British for too long to either want or be able to let go; always the hope spurred us on that despite appearances to the contrary it might all be a big pretence. One day they would admit they had been bled white and couldn't go on, and ask us for peace. We

117

recognized too the risk Germany ran of bleeding to death in the attempt.

The mission was demanding, much more of a strain than earlier voyages. We approached the coast at dawn, settled on the bottom and spent the long summer days in wait submerged. When evening fell we retired offshore, surfacing during the dark to breathe fresh sea air and recharge the electric batteries. Even then we remained in a state of maximum alertness, scouring the black horizons for a target, ever anxious not to miss anything. At first we had no luck. Two or three chances offered themselves, but proved beyond our reach. Another few days and a northbound convoy came thrashing up. I sank a steamer in exchange for an unpleasant depth-charging by the escorts. Two days later I torpedoed an oil tanker through a destroyer screen and another depth charge attack of unbelievable ferocity followed. We lurked on the bottom for several more fruitless days. How paradisial those free chases of the early war years now seemed in comparison to this miserable existence submerged!

Physically we suffered hardship. While above us the British basked in the glorious warmth of a hot July, we spent the summer days waiting on the sea bed, the boat as cold as an ice cellar, the interior ironwork dripping like a deep limestone cave. We all had rheumatism and were clad like eskimos. I wore several thick woollen scarves and sweaters and three pairs of trousers but it made no difference, I was always chilled to the bone.

At last, on 19 July 1918, we sighted not just a convoy but the biggest I had ever set eyes on – an armada steaming nonchalantly southwards and all I had to do was press the firing button when the first sacrifices arrived. Everything that happened that day will live for ever in my memory. Soon I observed the strength of the convoy defences, particularly the large numbers of destroyers preceding it. Its flanks were protected by countless small naval vessels and pinnaces. In the air was a barrage balloon, plus three aircraft. Should I watch the convoy upwards, sideways, ahead or astern? It wasn't so easy after all. I had to manoeuvre gingerly and make sure I kept well down.

118

I took station directly below a destroyer. In two minutes I intended to attack with all four bow torpedoes. I made a 360-degree sweep with the periscope. There was a naval vessel coming up from my stern, whether it was a destroyer or pinnace I could not determine. Had he seen us or was his approach coincidental? He was very close now. For safety I called into the control room, "Go to 20 metres quickly!"

Assuming a bow-heavy attitude the boat inclined deeper at once. Shortly before the fore-end reached the twenty metre mark the hydroplanes were set to trim the boat in the horizontal position. At the same instant there was a suspiciously familiar exterior noise, followed by a short series of tremendous explosions as three depth charges went off one after the other very close to the hull. Immediately the engine-room reported serious flooding and it was found that the hydroplanes were immoveable in the "rise" position. The boat was thus stern-heavy and losing depth. All hands stampeded to the bow and the regulating tanks were flooded in a futile attempt to restore the trim. The boat broke surface with the tower and prow protruding from the water.

"Flood all tanks!" I shouted. "It doesn't matter how, but get them flooded!" The boat continued to lay motionless on the surface. I questioned the control room repeatedly, "Are you flooding the tanks? Are all vents open?" and was perplexed to receive all manner of reassurances, since the boat was not submerging in the least and I could not fathom the reason.

A peep through the periscope provided me with a turbulent picture. We were wallowing at the centre of a ring of destroyers and armed pinnaces which were all machine-gunning the boat with various calibres. Suddenly the firing stopped. I circled with the periscope and saw a destroyer closing in to ram from the port beam. I bellowed a warning into the control room and for a few seconds we braced ourselves for the inevitable. When it came, there was a grinding crunch so powerful that I feared it would roll the boat over. This did not happen although the fore section was severely damaged.

UB-110 was now undiveable. The hydroplanes were jammed; the dive tanks could not be flooded: therefore the boat was lost.

119

All that remained was to ensure that the crew was saved.

"Blow all tanks!" I roared. The boat rose a little so that all hatches were just above the surface. And now I gave the most difficult order of my life, "Abandon the boat!", before descending into the control room in order to be the last man to leave.

I ordered Oberleutnant Loebell, who was still in the conning tower, to open the bridge hatch, which he was unable to do. I sent one of the engine room men to help him to no avail; the lid would not budge. I went up myself and got it open eventually, since I knew its little peculiarities. The cover opened with a loud clang and the air pressure from within the boat ripped off my service cap and sent it sailing into the air in a high arc.

The crew were thronging below me on the ladder and I could not return below. So I stood on the bridge beside the hatch so that at least I would still be last to leave the tower.

Quickly I surveyed the situation. The boat had a list of at least 15° to starboard where the depth charges had ripped open the dive tanks on that side. We were in an inferno of noise, surrounded by destroyers and small armed escort craft which maintained a relentless fire on us, while overhead two of the three aircraft were circling menacingly. I felt like a spectator at some gigantic outdoor theatre. I glanced up at the two aircraft and noticed that they had also begun shooting. Loebell was wounded inside the conning tower, hit by a steel splinter; meanwhile the crew was leaving the boat. I counted the heads: nobody was missing. Everybody bar the commander and watchkeeping officers wore a lifejacket.

I watched as a destroyer built up speed for a fresh ramming manoeuvre. At the last moment I jumped into the sea to protect myself against the force of the impact. With great presence of mind Förster, one of the engine room hands, leapt up and caught the railing chains of the destroyer. When he attempted to clamber aboard, a British Petty Officer struck him so brutally on the hands with a revolver that he fell back into the sea.

At this point I blacked out momentarily and when I regained consciousness I found myself swimming. *UB-110* was nowhere to be seen. The ramming had sunk her. The destroyer was hove to nearby. My crew was in the water waiting to be picked up. But there was indiscipline aboard the British ship. Men from the destroyer's engine room fired on the survivors with revolvers, while others hurled large lumps of coal at the heads in the water. The smaller armed craft had closed in meanwhile and were also exercising their machine gunners. Above the fearful chatter of the MGs and revolvers screams of pain could be heard.

A little way away my 18-year-old steward, blond Arndt, a miner by occupation, looked towards me imploringly without making a sound. I realized that he was exhausted. I had started to swim towards him when his skull was split open by a large lump of coal. He was dead before I got to him. Shortly after, Oberleutnant Loebell, who was swimming nearby and had no lifejacket, said that he had been shot in the thigh and was having difficulty in treading water to remain afloat. I gave him support by holding up the waistband of his trousers. "Let me die in peace," he said. "The swine are going to murder us all anyway." I made no reply and merely held on to him.

By now the merchant convoy was in our vicinity and the shooting at the survivors tailed off abruptly. What saved us was the presence of the neutral ships in the convoy. As if by magic the British now let down some lifeboats into the water. I dragged Loebell up to one and heaved him over the gunwale. I still had some energy left and preferred to be last out of the water if possible. I felt my strength ebbing and made for a small escort craft lying stopped in the water. I was struck a fearful blow on the back of the head and lost consciousness again. I regained my senses almost at once and saw that I had been run down by the stem of a lifeboat. I felt a hand grasp my collar and a voice invited me to lift myself aboard – "Come on, old chap!" – but I was too weak and in the end the British had to haul me in themselves.

Six of my crew were in the lifeboat. I asked the British helmsman to pick up my Chief Engineer who was drifting past. He was supported by his lifejacket, his head sunk on his chest. They dragged him aboard and tried some artificial respiration without success. The body was then put in the bow of the boat.

121

The lifeboat put back towards the destroyer. On the way the helmsman asked, "Where is the captain?" My men pointed to me without speaking. The helmsman shook his head in disbelief. It was a fortnight since I last washed and shaved and I looked like a vagrant. I had abandoned my reefer jacket and seaboots in the water and was wearing only a filthy sweater and leather trousers, both saturated; my hair straggled down my face. The helmsman shouted to the destroyer that he had the U-boat captain aboard. A rope ladder was lowered over the side of the destroyer and I was the first to clamber up.

At the top an officer and two men stood waiting. The officer said, "Hands up!" and while the two ratings each covered me with a pistol the officer searched my pockets and confiscated the contents. Then he ordered me to follow him. I was given dry clothing. After I had changed, a cup of tea and ship's biscuit was served. He said I should get something inside me, then we could have a little talk.

I observed that the destroyer had detached itself from the convoy and was now following the coast in a northerly direction. The officer, probably the officer of the watch, congratulated me: "For you, the war is over." He said it in a serious and respectful way as a prelude to the interrogation process.

"The war will last another two years before Britain wins."

"Really?"

"Britain is now building enormous war factories. With the material being produced in them, Germany will definitely feel the pinch at the latest by 1919."

"I see."

"Have you heard the latest news from the Western Front? The whole German line has pulled back!" I thought about this. In the last army communiqué we had picked up on the telegraphy receiver there had been mention of a planned retreat, and so it seemed likely that what the officer said was within the realms of possibility.

In my enormously excited and distraught mental state it all made a deep impression on me. The final minutes in *UB-110*: the thought of all the deaths and the manner of their dying, of the many fine men of my crew, the mad buzzing in my skull after the blow I had received on the back of my head. The best I could do in this state of mind was to refuse to answer. When the British officer saw my decision he terminated the interview. Late that afternoon we put into Newcastle and moored alongside an old accommodation ship some way up the Tyne.

I was led out on the destroyer's deck. The first thing I saw was the corpse of my Chief Engineer. I requested permission to examine the body. I had to know how this man, who had grown very dear to me, had met his end. Did he drown or had he been shot dead in the water? Permission was refused.

To my question how many of the thirty-four men whom I had counted leaving the conning tower of my boat had been saved, the British naval officer looked away and murmured, "Thirteen". I reminded myself that at all times I should maintain a military bearing and made no comment.

I was transferred to the accommodation ship and allocated a well-appointed cabin many decks down. The door remained open and a naval sentry with a sidearm was stationed outside. After about half an hour I was led out for a second interrogation by the ship's captain. It seemed probable that great store was set on getting these interviews under way as soon as possible after capture when the prisoner would be off his guard and still unsettled. I saw that the important thing now was to remain noncommittal.

The interviewing officer had before him a book entitled *Instructions for the Interrogation of German U-boat Crews*. Presumably having found the replies to his opening remarks unsatisfactory, he opened the book, glanced through it and then asked me, "Please tell me, how old were the most recent newspapers you had on board?"

"I had none."

"But supposing you did have some, how old would they have been?"

"I had forbidden the bringing of newspapers aboard my boat. At sea it is important for every man to concentrate on his duties. There was no time for reading newspapers."

The obvious purpose of these questions was to establish our sailing date. A number of questions in like vein followed but my answers were as evasive as the questions and the interview was soon aborted. A second session later proved equally futile.

I remained aboard the accommodation ship and was treated extremely well. The meals were far better than standard fare for years in Germany: white tinned bread, fruit of all kinds, jam and marmalade, thick slices of roast beef, all served with a demeanour that suggested they were available in plenty. The British officers went to any length to make me feel at home, being frequently on hand to talk about any subject under the sun, and they would never go off without leaving me some reading material.

Meanwhile I had had to return the clothing I had been given by the sub-lieutenant of the destroyer. I received in exchange a parcel from the Shipwrecked Mariners' Society, the contents of which did nothing to enhance my appearance. This was supplemented later by an issue of fatigues complete with a "sixpence cap".

The accommodation ship was moored about fifty metres from a bank of the Tyne and through a convenient porthole I was able to watch the comings and goings at the landing stage. On the morning of the second day I noticed a large crowd beginning to congregate. Later an armed troop of British soldiers arrived and erected barricades between the crowd and the exit of the landing stage. The naval officer of the watch appeared and told me to pack; I was to be taken to London with the six crewmen who had been with me in the lifeboat. The other seven survivors of the boat had already been taken to London by another route.

I followed my naval sentry to the upper deck, fell in at the centre of the squad of infantry, marched to the accommodation ladder, boarded a boat with the six others and was rowed ashore. On disembarking, the crowd, which was probably composed of fisherfolk, broke out into loud howls and whistles. We could hardly blame them for their expression of hatred for U-boatmen, since we had deprived so many of them of their boats and livelihoods through our activities all along the English east coast. We realized now that the large armed escort was more for our protection than to prevent our escape; if the crowd got really ugly we might easily have been lynched. The soldiers could not defend us against a shower of rotten eggs, fish and sputum; we endured a ghastly fifteen minutes of it between the landing stage and the railway station. My relief to be safely seated in a carriage can be imagined.

My army officer escort was most attentive, asking if he could buy me some reading matter, was I hungry and did I need a cup of tea. I could see that these inquiries were an unspoken apology for the behaviour of the mob. I acknowledged his kindness but politely declined every offer.

Between six and seven that evening the train came to a halt in a large and sooty London terminus. On alighting in the company of the army officer I was at once accosted by a tall British naval officer, clean-shaven, with red hair and small fanatical eyes who said to me in fluent German, "Good evening, Herr Fürbringer, I am glad you are here at last, we have been waiting for you for so long."

A police van was waiting in the station forecourt. In the custody of armed soldiers I was driven to the detention barracks in Hyde Park near the Kensington Museum where all German airmen and U-boat officers spent a few weeks in solitary confinement for interrogation purposes. I was allocated a single cell, bare except for a small wooden washstand, a rolled mattress and a bucket.

In an ironical tone an army provost-sergeant invited me to "make myself comfortable".

"Well, before I do," I replied, "would you like to get me something to eat?" He said he didn't know if that were possible, but a few minutes later he reappeared and dropped two slices of bread on the washstand. Once he had gone I fell on them, ravenous with hunger. Within seconds the two slabs, hard as concrete, had vanished.

The next day I was re-quartered in a better cell furnished with a proper table and a coconut mat. Adequate quantities of porridge and tea were served. Although I had grown accustomed to having a guard close by, I found it more irritating to be the subject of constant inspection through a spy-hole in the cell door.

At about 11 o'clock I was brought to a room for another interrogation. I was welcomed by the naval officer who had met me at King's cross station the previous evening. In a debonair manner he invited me to be seated, offered me a cigarette which I declined and then proposed that I supply my career details since entering the Imperial Navy. I obliged him for the period prior to the outbreak of war.

"Beyond that," I explained, "I am unable to say anything since all my experiences during the war are classified as secret."

"Oh, but they are not secret," he contradicted.

"Oh yes they are."

"Oh no they are not."

This stupid exchange continued like a tennis rally.

"I am sorry, but clearly you have misunderstood German military law as to what is, and what is not, secret," I insisted firmly after the seventh exchange.

"I think I know German military law better than you do, Kapitänleutnant Fürbringer, and I assure you your wartime experiences are not secret."

"Look, I'm not going to argue about it, you'll just have to take my word for it."

"Never let it be said that I would argue with a German officer," he countered. We sat and stared at each other for two minutes. A cigarette was offered afresh. He asked my opinion about the sinking of the *Lusitania*. When he had my answer he replied that if he had his way I would be hanged as a pirate. There was a long silence before he spoke again.

"Which boats of the Flanders Flotilla are at sea now?"

"How should I know?"

"Do you think Maxe got back safely?"

No answer. But how did he know the pet name of U-boat commander Max Viebeg? Maxe would probably have sailed just after I did. I was amazed that this man should know such intimate details.

"If you could be a little more forthcoming," he suggested, "I could get you much better treatment. For example, I could put you in touch with Seppl."

"Seppl?"

126

"Yes, Seppl Weninger. Lala too if you like."

I suppressed a gasp. Lala was my friend Kapitänleutnant Lafranz. This British officer knew a lot, perhaps everything. But from where? What he was saying literally took my breath away. Now I was warned to say nothing whatever, secret or not secret.

"Who sank the hospital ship in the Irish Sea? Was it Amberger or someone else?" he threw at me.

From where did he get all this? I asked myself repeatedly. It was possible that he had craftily tricked the information from other German prisoners. As officers we had not allowed our thoughts to contemplate the possibility of capture and our crewmen had not been instructed on the pitfalls to avoid while under interrogation. When I heard this officer speak so freely about Seppl, Lala and Amberger it dawned on me suddenly that the British espionage system in Bruges must be far more efficient than any of us had ever suspected. This man spoke as though he had been among us in the mess, listening to our chatter. If only I could get a message of warning to Bruges from here!

The interrogation was terminated. I met his final request for information in exchange for improved treatment with a stony silence and was led away. Seldom had I experienced such a depressing sixty minutes and never previously had Germany's innocence as to the underground ferreting out of information and war secrets been made so alarmingly clear to me.

I spent almost four weeks in solitary confinement. During that time I was allowed to write one letter to my wife, which failed to arrive, and pass the time gazing at the distant thoroughfare. Breakfast was always tolerable but the catering was otherwise utterly deplorable. The midday meal was normally a decomposing salted herring with three small potatoes. The provost sergeant served it up every day with the comment, "Well, I don't know about you but I couldn't eat it."

Only twice was I allowed exercise in the fresh air. On the second occasion in Hyde Park an old lady, suddenly confronted by my gaunt, dogged, unshaved face gasped, "Oh, you're the most beast-like man I ever saw!" I knew I made an unprepossessing sight, but to induce in an old lady a feeling of horror

127

was more than I could have expected. For amusement I made a
grimace, but she had seen enough already. She turned her back
to me and for a moment as I stared at her ample posterior I
knew that the U-boat food blockade of Britain had failed. The
two sergeants escorting me gave me a grin and, almost as if
reading my mind, nodded in sympathy.

Chapter 12

COLSTERDALE

I was held for four weeks in the Detention Barracks, four gruelling weeks in solitary confinement, beset by agonizing worries and a sense of grinding outrage. But all things come to an end, and one day I was reunited with my watchkeeping officers Loebell and Tietze for the journey north to the officers' camp at Colsterdale. After everything we had endured the emotional occasion of the reunion is something I would prefer to gloss over, but at least the morale of my companions had not sunk to the depths mine had reached, probably because they had shared a cell throughout. The journey with company provided me with spiritual uplift, but at first I had a difficult period in the camp itself adjusting to being amongst so many.

Colsterdale, at Masham, near Manchester, was the officers' prison camp that would be my world for God only knew how long. It was situated in a rough, hilly and treeless heathland, exposed to a fierce wind which blew often. When it rained, as it frequently did, the clouds hugged the featureless landscape which I found curiously depressing, but the place had its charm when the sun shone and the climate, healthy despite its raw side, was not unpleasant once one had grown accustomed to it.

There were two camps, North and South, to hold respectively 250 and 500 German officers of all branches of service. Most of us were lodged in North Camp; initially there were only twenty officers in South Camp. Three of these were U-boat commanders. The camps were well organized, the barracks were clean and German non-commissioned ranks served us. One remembers the first days as being almost pleasant. Everyone had his story to tell of the events leading up to his capture. When the endless storytelling began to pall we contemplated bettering our existence. The most important thing seemed to be sport. The canteen sold no food or drink, only laces, belts and so on. We ordered hockey equipment and for a while took up the game in earnest until we realized that we were too malnourished to participate in energetic activities.

Colsterdale filled up suddenly. Drafts of fifty to one hundred officers appeared. North Camp was soon full and the rest were allocated to South Camp. Newly arrived army officers described the great land battles on the Western Front during which they had been captured. Their morale was not good. They wore healthy tans and looked fit but psychologically they were in poor condition. Certainly the loss of freedom resulted in an inclination to view things on the black side but these officers were almost in an anxiety state. What appalled them most was the material superiority of the Allies. Repeatedly they spoke of the enemy tank forces: how the tanks broke through the German lines and rolled them up; how the enemy infantry was transported on the tanks; how our German troops, especially the newer recruits, were simply overcome by the strength and apparent invulnerability of the Allied tanks. We breathed a sigh of relief when a later draft of prisoners provided descriptions which all tallied, suggesting that German troops were now tackling the tank problem more effectively, although the enemy remained superior on the Front because of his advantage in massed tanks. The presence of battalion and regimental commanders among the prisoners proved the speed and depth of penetration behind our lines, a fact which these higher ranking officers confirmed. All officers were highly critical of the pitiful standard of catering at the Front and of the low quality of manpower now arriving from Germany. Industry had so far been unable to supply in sufficient quantity the 6-cm anti-tank trench gun which had proved exceptionally valuable. It was often stated that the High Command had no proper appreciation of the conditions at the Front, otherwise they would long ago have pulled back certain exhausted units into reserve unless – and this was the question which made us all edgy – the pressure on the Front was already so strong that they could not afford to rest them.

As for the Americans, about whose virtues we often enquired, the Western Front officers were more sanguine. They reported that attacks by US troops were beaten off easily, although recently there were signs of a greater tenacity as they adapted to warfare.

I must say that it was an exasperating experience to have become a mere partisan spectator after having participated actively for so long in these affairs. My existence now seemed superfluous.

Together with a number of the long-term PoWs I was transferred to a quieter area of the camp where few officers were quartered. It lay high on a slope. On the hilltop there was a sports field which we used later, after regaining our strength.

How were the endless hours in camp to be put to profitable use? The idea of writing my war experiences appealed, but the British confiscated these personal diaries whenever they found them and so we settled for chess, cards and reading newspapers. Nearly every officer had a regular order for the latter. I took the *Manchester Guardian* because it took a much fairer line towards Germany than the others. Nevertheless, what we read was not encouraging.

Elections were held for camp administrative functionaries. These positions were much sought after since they offered regular employment. I ranked equivalent to an Army *Hauptmann* but had less service than any of them and so an office eluded me. I bought some English books, mostly histories, sent off to Germany for others and read daily until my eyes ached. I never stopped, otherwise I dwelt on other matters and became morbid.

Soon a number of scholarly officers ran courses: physics, chemistry, mathematics, languages (especially English and French) and so on. I was fascinated by the philosophy lectures of Dr Scheller.

My greatest fear was that captivity might inflict upon me lasting spiritual and psychological damage, and so I kept myself as busy as possible, never pausing to accept the idea that I was not a free man, that I had the life of a mere drone while across the water others fought on. But it was not an easy fact to ignore. Repeatedly I asked myself, "What point is there in learning philosophy? While Germany is engaged in a life and death struggle for all we hold dear, and needs all hands to the pumps, here you are reading philosophy of all things, which can do nothing to help!"

Fortunately for my state of mind the *Hauptmann* functionary of the catering administration was suddenly transferred to South Camp and I was elected in his stead. My darkest thoughts were cast aside at last. I was now a sort of spokesman for the whole camp. Catering was the most important of all camp affairs; all had the keenest interest on what went on and no funny business. Every item of food was strictly rationed, literally to the last potato, the last spoonful of sugar and the last pinch of salt.

All in all the food was tolerable, although at first we had no salt. This was bad, but if it was a sign that the British were short of salt due to the U-boat blockade, it was good. After several weeks, to our chagrin, a great surplus of the condiment was delivered to the kitchen. A bitter salt indeed!

The British supplied the food but we had to cook it. It was my duty to inspect and approve the supply and to exercise the most meticulous exactitude in the distribution. For this purpose I had the assistance of three naval lieutenants and several kitchen ADCs.

We received a meat allowance, usually horse flesh, three times per week, the ADCs having to drag half a horse, the purplish, gristly flesh of which looked anything but appetizing, down the hillside and into the kitchen mincer. Although it was said to taste quite good, many of us were unable to overcome our prejudice against eating horse and we traded our portions for potatoes.

It was one of my duties as catering functionary to be present in the dining hall after the food had been served. When I entered

132

the hall on the first day when horse meat appeared on the menu the entire assembly began to whinny. I rang the meal bell to request silence and stated that, whereas I did not mind the neighing, anyone who kicked out would be confined to his stable for a fortnight. The officers whinnied their acceptance.

What the British supplied – potatoes, rice, noodles, porridge oats, condensed milk and coffee – was of good quality but in short supply. Polster, a kitchen lieutenant, produced a recipe for a sort of biscuit baked from porridge oats and sweetened egg white, the pride of the cooks, and it was always a red letter day when *Polsterkuchen* appeared on the menu. From the canteen, run by an English civilian, we were able to purchase a weak cider which would make you drunk if you could get enough of it, but it required an effort.

Often it was a hopeless task to distribute the portions fairly. Potatoes come in all sizes and I had the difficult task of ensuring that each table received the same number and weight of potatoes. Each officer watched me like a hawk. To avoid friction I instituted a system in which table spokesmen attended regular conferences to express the opinions of their respective table members. These meetings were a safety valve and restored harmony. Differences were better resolved on a council basis than on a stage in front of 250 hungry stomachs. The time soon came when the system ran itself and less of my time was spent refereeing and catering.

In time the British increased the daily ration that some of us with relatives in the neutral countries began to receive, gifts of food, even large crates of tinned meat. From my elder brother interned in Holland I had the first news of home in a note concealed inside a packet of cigarettes.

So passed the months of September and October 1918. I will never forget the day when we heard of the defeat of Bulgaria. The British counted us three times per day, after breakfast, in the evening around six o'clock and in bed between ten and eleven o'clock. On 23 September, during the second count in the dining hall, the British sergeant-major bent forward and whispered a few words to Kapitänleutnant Morath, the Senior German Officer, who blanched and stood up. As soon as the

British warrant officer had left the hall, Morath announced what he had been told: Bulgaria had capitulated. We were utterly dismayed. We knew that the Bulgarian situation was difficult but had not prepared for a disaster on this scale. Morath and I shared a room and long into the early hours we discussed the implications of the Bulgarian defeat. It was clear that the Allied forces had won a valuable propaganda victory and that it now required little less than a miracle for our side to redress the balance. Privately we admitted that whatever Germany might still be capable of achieving on the various Fronts and in the U-boat war, it would not be enough to change our military fortunes. That night we acknowledged that defeat was now inevitable. As the morning dawned, we fell into a troubled sleep.

The morning newspaper delivery brought a grim confirmation. We did not believe everything of course, but what we knew was true was enough. The collapse began, presaged by the deteriorating morale on the Home Front and in the general attitude of hopelessness conveyed to the Front by fresh reinforcements. Next followed the resignation of Ludendorff and the German peace offer leading to the Armistice and the abdication and exile of the Kaiser to Holland. I saw horror and pain on every face as we knew defeat. Then came the Red Revolution. One of the kitchen lieutenants, a schoolteacher from Bavaria, tore off his epaulettes and avowed brotherhood with the cooks, who then laid down their utensils. The British arrived and said that whoever was still on strike in five minutes would be court-martialled for refusing labour. This put an end to the nonsense. Everything was soon straightened out. I think it was a kind of PoW madness. Captivity and the dreadful tidings from home drove a man out of his senses.

The worst day for all German naval officers was to learn that the Fleet had sailed to Britain as war reparations. It seemed to augur ill that the ships had not been scuttled in German waters beforehand: we had begun to hear alien phrases such as "soldiers' councils" and "workers' soviets" in letters from home, which, though written in the most guarded terms, hinted at the alarming political trend clearly enough.

Then the sergeant-major newsbringer whispered to Kapitänleutnant Morath, "Your ships have scuttled themselves in Scapa Flow." How breathlessly we waited the papers on the morning of 22 June 1919 and devoured the details of the honourable destruction of the High Seas Fleet on the previous day!

Subsequent to the Armistice there was no change in our handling or treatment. It had invariably been fair in any case, as was merited by our exemplary discipline. Up to the summer of 1919 the drear diet of dead horse and the bacon of pigs fed on fish continued. We were all seriously emaciated. With the improvement, apples and nuts arrived in the canteen.

The exercise period was restricted to two or three hours twice weekly, being a brisk walk in single file with an officer at the head and a sergeant bringing up the rear. The landscape was so barren that no opportunity presented itself for someone to slip away unnoticed. Because of the efficient camp security, the thrice daily count and the tight watch maintained at the coast, escape seemed altogether impossible.

The one and only escape was made by two 19-year-old officers in May 1919. All North Camp knew that the attempt was to be made and we did everything we could to help, although we remained doubtful about their chances of success.

The gates to the sports field on the hilltop were left open between ten in the morning and five in the afternoon. When closed the compound was not guarded. A sports day had been agreed with the British camp authorities for the day of the planned escape. In the middle of the field a long-jump sandpit had been dug. This would be raked over and smoothed with a spade after each competitor had jumped.

At the appropriate moment towards five o'clock, each of the three sentries was distracted by a small pantomime and a crowd suddenly formed in a circle around the sandpit to obscure the excavation of two shallow trenches and the two escapers, wearing civilian clothes made up by the German camp tailor, laid down and were quickly buried with a light covering of sand. The sporting events having finished, we marched out of the arena. A British officer and two sergeants made a brief check

135

to ensure that nobody had been left behind, sealed off the sports field and dismissed the sentries.

We had the task of concealing the escape from the British authorities. The first count was at six o'clock that evening. The dining hall was divided into two rooms, one large and one small, by means of a wooden partition, and the prisoners were counted while eating. The two escapees had their places in the small room. The partition was the weak point of the counting system. A small two-way catflap had been cut into the partition sufficiently large for a person to crawl through. After having been counted in the large room, while the attention of the British counting staff was distracted two officers passed into the smaller room via the flap and were included in the small room count.

It was the practice to count us in bed between ten and eleven in the evening. The escapers' bunks, draped with underwear and clothing from the bunk above, were occupied by dummies with straw heads topped with a mop of barber's sweepings. This was also successful.

The most difficult count to cheat was held in the morning in the large room of the dining hall. There were twelve barracks; each barrack formed a squad of three rows. The first squad was counted and each officer also had to answer his name when the register was called. When this had been accomplished satisfactorily, the squad made a right turn and marched out of the hall. The next barrack was not counted until the previous squad was clear of the hall. Two sentries were posted outside the doors to ensure that no funny business occurred. Theoretically this counting system was foolproof but as the British were not aware of the catflap in the wooden partition, two officers with voices similar to those of the escapees entered the unwatched small room from the outside and used the flap to join the appropriate squad for the falsification of the count.

The cover-up was never detected. At eleven o'clock on the morning of the fourth day all prisoners were ordered to the sports field for an emergency count and the deficiency was discovered. Apparently the camp administration had received information from the police at Hull docks that two men arrested there claimed to be escaped PoWs from Colsterdale North.

The two escapees had arrived at Hull without problems. Neither spoke much English but from the canteen they had somehow obtained money and this was used for food. They slept outdoors. At Hull, posing as Dutch seamen, they made enquiries for a ship to Holland but when questioned by a constable neither was able to produce a seaman's discharge book to substantiate the story and they were arrested.

The pair were returned the following day and received several weeks' solitary confinement. Their adventure had done them good, however, and the British took the affair in good part. They pressurized the Senior German Officer, Morath, for the methods used but as far as I know they were never disclosed.

At Colsterdale the British took the influenza epidemic of 1919 very seriously and every room was disinfected daily with lysol. This had a dreadful stench but no German prisoner contracted the virus. On the other hand eight of the British camp guards died of it.

Daily we waited for news of our mass repatriation. The worries of continued separation from family troubled us greatly. The months went by. There was no world but that within the barbed wire perimeter. Was it for their amusement or had we been forgotten by the victors? We grew more irritable and difficult to handle. Repeatedly the British officers confided that it would be soon, although in all probability they knew as much as we did. To crown it all Morath and I received notification that we would be held back for trial as war criminals. To be told this in the midst of repatriation fever was the bitterest blow that could befall us. The date for the mass departure was announced for 19 November 1919. As nothing more had been mentioned about a trial Morath and I packed along with the others. On 16 November we were called before the camp commandant and told to pack ready for transport to London where we would be subjected to a judicial interrogation. I wonder still if there ever was any such intention on the part of the British authorities. Perhaps it was all a joke or a form of revenge for all their ships we had sunk.

137

On 18 November Morath and I were sent for again to receive notice of our repatriation to Germany. Next day we boarded a German steamer at Hull. Once the English coast had receded from sight we made the sign of the cross three times for our safe delivery. I stepped ashore at Wilhelmshaven where I had spent the first day of the Great War. But meanwhile what changes had come to pass in poor Germany!

EPILOGUE

Großadmiral Tirpitz, Commander-in-Chief of the Germany Navy, resigned on 15 March 1916 in protest at the undertaking by his Government not to engage in unrestricted submarine warfare at a time when the naval blockade of Germany had brought the issue to a head. What was required by the German Admiralty was no less than the reinstatement of Admiral von Pohl's order of February 1915. But in the critical period when the judgement of battle hung in the balance, von Bethmann-Hollweg's Government wanted to spare all neutral shipping, and could not be dissuaded. The U-boats had been obliged to continue the offensive at sea while subject to a large range of restrictions, and, unable to develop their potential to the full, had conceded the initiative to powerful enemy counter-measures by the time when all encumbrances were lifted in February 1917.

A few months after his return to Germany and discharge from naval service in the rank of Kapitänleutnant, Werner Fürbringer took a position with Blohm & Voss, the large Hamburg shipyard which had built his later commands. "Even for a man with employment the postwar prospects in a defeated Germany were grim," he informed his 1933 readership, "so I emigrated, first to the Netherlands, then Turkey." But the truth of the matter was that whereas Germany was supposed to have no further interest in U-boat warfare, Fürbringer was one of the pioneers of the emergent but clandestine U-boat Arm from its earliest beginnings.

Under absolute duress, Germany was a signatory to the Peace Treaty of Versailles on 28 June 1919. By virtue of Article 191 of the Treaty, Germany was prohibited from building, acquiring or operating submarines of any description. The Allies had not confiscated the valuable U-boat designs and blueprints and, under the auspices of the newly formed Reichsmarine, a consortium of former U-boat builders set up a company known as NV *Ingenieurskantoor voor Scheepsbouw*, a drawing office in a Dutch shipyard offering comprehensive expertise in submarine development and construction to aspirant naval powers. The principal clients consulting IvS were Japan, Italy, Spain, Sweden and Argentina (in the latter republic, Karl Bartenbach, the former CO of the Flanders U-boat Flotilla, advised on the creation of its submarine force). The plans all bearing the signatures of Techel and Schürer, men who had achieved fame in the Great War, covered a range of Types. Two boats, a 250-tonner at Abo, Finland for the Finnish Navy and a 500-tonner at Cadiz for the Turks, were built for the private account of the Dutch firm. During this period, Werner Fürbringer was in Holland.

In 1926, when Turkey placed a large order for submarines to be built at Rotterdam under German engineering and technical supervision, 'retired' U-boat commanders such as Werner Fürbringer acted in an advisory capacity. Before delivery of the completed vessels to Turkey in March 1928, German crews gained useful experience by putting the boats through extensive trials. The boats created the need for a training school in Turkey and in due course German crews were shipped out to attend clandestine courses. During this period Werner Fürbringer was in Turkey.

He returned to Germany in 1931 and in the Spring of 1932 made a lecture tour addressing German youth on the subject of U-boat warfare. Between then and Christmas 1933 he fulfilled a civilian overseas appointment to train U-boat volunteers aboard one of the three new submarines delivered by IvS to the Finnish Navy in 1930.

The manuscript for his memoir *Alarm! Tauchen!!* was delivered to the Berlin publishing house of Ullstein in the autumn of 1932 and was published the following year. If the book can be considered part and parcel of a U-boat recruiting drive it is interesting that he should have depicted U-boat life as such an arduous and miserable form of existence. He did not understate the personnel losses, and placed blame for the Kaiser's failure at sea squarely on the political leadership and its advisers.

Fürbringer re-entered the German Navy in 1933 with the rank of Korvettenkapitän and was appointed Senior Instructor at the Kiel-Wik 'Anti-submarine School' which was of course exactly the reverse of what its title stated.

At the outbreak of war in September 1939 he held the post of Senior Planning Officer, U-boats, at the Oberkommando der Marine (OKM), and was Assistant to Admiral Raeder's Chief of Staff, Admiral Schniewind. He retired from the Kriegsmarine in the rank of Konteradmiral in 1943 but in that year he was still only 55 years of age. A sequel to his earlier volume based on experiences and opinions at Staff level might have proved very informative. His decorations included the Iron Cross First and Second Class and the Order of the House of Hohenzollern with Swords.

Regarding the alleged British atrocity committed against survivors of UB-110, the normal procedure would have been to report the matter to the German legal military authorities at the earliest opportunity. Depositions would then have been taken from all available witnesses. One can imagine how far it would have proceeded subsequently. It is not, and never has been, the practice of the British military authorities to try British service personnel for alleged war crimes committed against enemy belligerents in wartime no matter how strong the evidence.

Werner Fürbringer died in Braunschweig on 8 February 1982 at the age of 91. At the time of publication he is survived by a daughter and two sons.

INDEX

143

145